Whales & Man

Whales & Man

Adventures with the Giants of the Deep

By Tim Dietz

Illustrations by Grace Goldberg

YANKEE BOOKS

A division of Yankee Publishing Incorporated
Dublin, N.H.

Edited by Dougald MacDonald
Designed by Eugenie Seidenberg

First Edition
Copyright 1987 by Yankee Publishing Incorporated

Library of Congress Catalogue Card Number: 86-51013

ISBN: 0-89909-120-2

To Kathy, Lani, and Erin
and our adventures together.

Acknowledgments

There are many individuals — too numerous to mention — who helped make this book possible, and to all of them I give thanks for their thoughtful comments and efforts. I owe special thanks to Bob Gowell and Roy Morejon of the National Marine Fisheries Service in Portland, Maine, and to Connie Veilleux and Brett Baker for their enthusiastic help; to Chuck Nicklin, Hal Whitehead, Debbie Glockner-Ferrari, Howard Hall, Mike Williamson, Rich Sears, Charles "Stormy" Mayo, Flip Nicklin, Peter Chorney, Sheridan Stone, Butch Huntley, and Richard Stanford for their fascinating interviews; to Clarissa Silitch and the staff at Yankee Books for their enthusiastic support; to my editor, Dougald MacDonald, for his patience and skillful mastery of the written word; to Sharon Smith and Eugenie Seidenberg for their behind-the-scenes, but truly appreciated, efforts; to David Mishkin of The Photo Finish in Portland, Maine, for his help with photo processing; and to Grace Goldberg for her dedication and commitment to creating the beautiful illustrations for this book. Most of all, I owe my deepest love and thanks to my dear wife, Kathy, and our daughter, Lani, for their love and support during the many months "Daddy" spent typing in seclusion upstairs. Their love is my inspiration.

Table of Contents

INTRODUCTION

I stood in the meager light of a streetlamp over the dock, shuffling soft gravel into mounds with my toe. Around me the hum of activity increased as the crew of the *M/V Yankee Freedom* readied the ship. Ahead lay a journey into the open waters of the western North Atlantic, into the heart of the spectacular ocean realm of the sperm whale.

For years I had photographed the whales of the Gulf of Maine, but I had never ranged beyond about 40 miles offshore. This trip would be dramatically different. Our route would take us 200 miles out of the port of Gloucester, Massachusetts, around the tip of Cape Cod, through the unpredictable waters over Georges Bank to our ultimate destination: Oceanographer Canyon, a submarine valley that cuts through the outer continental shelf to the depths beyond. In all, we would spend three days exploring a foreign and beautiful world.

Although it was nearing 10 P.M., an hour when most people are preparing for a quiet night's sleep, the air dockside was energized with anticipation. Luggage and camera equipment piled up as expedition members trickled in. The weather, which for days I'd watched with uncommon zeal, was cooperating nicely. The air was unusually crisp and clear for late August, and the short-term forecast called for fair skies and gentle breezes. Spirits were high as we finally gathered our things and boarded the ship. By now all 40 expedition members were on hand, as well as the trip leaders from Cornell University's Shoals Marine Laboratory, New England Whale Watch, and Seafarers Expeditions.

As I glanced at the diverse faces, I couldn't help drawing parallels between this trip and whaling voyages of a century or more before. Both crews hoped to spot the elusive sperm whale, and like the crew of a whaling ship, we had gathered from different walks of life, total strangers sharing a common interest. Unlike whalers, however, we would return not with barrels of oil rendered from dead whales but with memories and photographs of whales alive at sea.

After staking out our bunks and meeting the captain and crew, we got underway, accompanied by the low hum of diesel engines and the slight roll of the Atlantic as we cleared Gloucester Harbor. Out of sight of the lights onshore, we watched a shimmering blanket of stars spread quietly overhead. The crisp night air and the ship's slow roll, together with the late hour, made sleep come easily.

By 6:30 the following morning the ship was buzzing with activity. Through the night we had cruised around the eastern hook of Cape Cod, maintaining our east-southeast heading for the southern part of Georges Bank. By breakfast we were 50 miles southeast of Nantucket, enjoying smooth seas and sunny skies.

Georges Bank is one of the richest fishing grounds on earth. Deep-water currents welling up to the surface and the outflow from distant rivers carry a variety of nutrients to the area, which are further blended by the moving winds and tides. This mixture nourishes tremendous concentrations of plankton, the free-floating microscopic plants and animals that feed many fish and whales. Georges Bank also has been a center of controversy, as oil companies battle environmental and civic groups for the right to exploit major oil and gas fields in the area, and American fishermen contest Canadians' rights to fish there. It was near these gravelly shoals that we hoped to find the sperm whale.

Before long that morning we sighted a large herd of long-finned pilot whales, their jet-black, melon-shaped heads looking much like giant oil bubbles breaking the surface. They were moving very slowly, accompanied by several small calves that sporadically slapped their tail flukes on the water's surface.

Pilot whales were named by European fishermen, who followed the cetaceans in the belief that the whales would lead them to great schools of herring. These toothed mammals, sometimes referred to as blackfish, may exceed 20 feet in length, and because they're a particularly gregarious mammal, they sometimes are found in herds ex-

ceeding several hundred animals. They were a delight to watch as we slowly paralleled their course, keeping a slight distance to avoid disturbing them.

The relaxed atmosphere following breakfast seemed to loosen everybody up, and I soon entered into conversation with a group gathered on the bow. There was Rich, the paralegal from Manhattan, an affable, talkative man in his mid-forties; Len, an elderly farmer and former small-town airport owner from Vermont, whose inner youth belied his 80 or so years; Frank, a quiet and friendly schoolteacher who looked as Irish as his roots in South Boston; and Dr. Watts, a retired clinical psychologist from Washington, D.C., who had spent little time at sea but had a lifelong interest in it. We were united by our fascination with whales and by our hope of seeing one of the sea's more elusive creatures, the sperm whale.

An hour after we sighted the herd of pilot whales, the water suddenly came alive with Atlantic bottlenosed dolphins, shooting through the water like dark gray torpedoes off both sides of the ship. Their speed mocked our meager 17 knots as they rocketed toward the bow, finally settling in the pressure wave there, much to the delight of those of us who had stationed ourselves on the pulpit. Below us swam one of the world's more familiar whales, known to millions from the TV show *Flipper*. Their adaptability to captivity and capacity to learn (their brains are larger than human brains) have made the bottlenosed dolphin a favorite at marine parks everywhere. Here in their natural environment they took on an elegance not seen in the flips and antics of aquarium shows. For several minutes they rode with us, occasionally glancing up to watch the watchers, until tiring of the game, they disappeared in the blink of an eye.

The dolphins' sudden appearance, and the slowly changing color of the water from emerald green to blue, indicated that we were approaching temperate waters, near the influence of the Gulf Stream.

Then, not 40 yards off the starboard bow, a

Risso's dolphin, commonly known as grampus.

herd of Risso's dolphins made an appearance; their whitish scarred heads glowed like blue lights below the surface. The herd consisted of about 50 whales, including many that displayed the streaky scars that lead cetologists to theorize that these dolphins may be unusually aggressive toward their own kind. The scars match the pattern of the animals' teeth, and the bodies of older males, which grow up to 14 feet long, may end up almost all white with scar tissue. For several minutes we watched them roll, slap the surface with their flukes, and occasionally breach; then we continued on our way.

Over the next several hours the sea seemed alive with creatures, as we sighted more bottlenosed dolphins and pilot whales, along with a sunfish, a blue shark, striped dolphins, sting rays, the ever-present variety of seabirds, and minke whales and finbacks as far as the eye could see, their tall blows exploding like cannon shots from the choppy sea as they surfaced to breathe. By late afternoon the water had changed from light blue to the dark indigo that indicated we had reached the edge of the outer continental shelf, where the waters are well over a mile deep.

In our pursuit of the sperm whale, we were now cruising the very same waters where, in 1712, Christopher "Kit" Hussey and his little sloop full of Nantucket whalemen may have first encountered and killed a sperm whale — all quite by accident. In autumn of that year Hussey and his crew were caught in a tremendous storm that drove them far off their usual whaling grounds near the shores of their island home. For many hours, perhaps days, Hussey ran before the howling winds and mountainous seas, until the storm abated enough for the sailors to notice enormous black creatures surfacing all around them. These gigantic creatures looked not at all like the familiar right whales off Nantucket. They had squarish heads with a single spout that arched forward, unlike the vertical spouts of the baleen whales near the New England coast. With a mixture of skill and luck, Hussey's crew managed to kill one of the great whales, lash it to the side of the sloop, and tow it home.

Hussey had blundered into a herd of sperm whales, many of which were the size of his 70-foot sloop. The whalers were familiar with the species — one had stranded on Nantucket some years earlier — and they knew of its rich oil. At that time they had thought it was an extremely rare whale, perhaps even a mutation. Hussey proved otherwise, however — a stroke of fortune for the islanders. In the years to come, he and other Nantucket whalers cruised the offshore waters in pursuit of the richest prize of all.

We knew we were in the right area, but as early evening approached, we hadn't yet shared in

Hussey's good fortune. We were cruising near the great Gulf Stream, which flows in wandering currents from the tropical waters of the Straits of Florida north along the coast of North America and across the wide Atlantic to Europe. The influences of the warm Gulf Stream were clearly visible: sporadic floats of sargassum (so named by Portuguese sailors, who thought the air-bladder floats of the weed looked like *salgazo,* or small grapes), flying fish bolting from the waters in our wake, and even a Portuguese man-of-war, its deadly tentacles plumbing the depths for its next unsuspecting victim.

We would not enter the Gulf Stream, however, because sperm whales are known to congregate along its edges. Indeed, Benjamin Franklin, whose scientific curiosity led him to study the Gulf Stream, discovered this fact from his cousin, a Nantucket sea captain named Timothy Folger. The captain told Franklin that sperm whales "keep to the side of it, but are not met within it."

Throughout the late afternoon I kept watch in front of the bridge with trip leaders Scott Mercer and Scott Marion, scanning the horizon until our eyes ached, hoping to catch a brief glimpse of our prey. Our vigil intensified when we heard the marine forecast received by Captain Dick Kieley, which called for 25- to 30-knot winds on Georges by morning, a report that undoubtedly meant rough seas and a shortened visit to the area.

By 7 P.M. my eyes needed a rest, so I decided to take a short break for dinner. By then almost everyone had gathered in the dining area, their faces reddened by the bright sun, their spirits soaring from the numerous sightings. I ate quickly and returned to the bridge to resume the vigil. Shortly afterward I was rejoined by Marion. By now the sun was just above the horizon. Suddenly, the quiet was shattered as Kevin McCarthy, who had been casually guiding the ship's wheel with his bare feet, knocked excitedly on the bridge window behind us. He was pointing directly off bow: "A sperm whale! A sperm whale!"

Forks, knives, and plates banged and clattered

as the dining room emptied in a scene reminiscent of the moment Gregory Peck and Richard Basehart first sighted the great white whale in the movie *Moby Dick.* The players in *this* scene, however, were grabbing for cameras and light meters instead of harpoons and lances.

Just off the bow a good-size sperm whale blew; its black, square head loomed above the surface like the bow of a massive submarine. The frenzied rush to the rail had now quieted to a hushed, almost reverent watch, disturbed only by the occasional click of a camera shutter. We drifted just past the giant, now silhouetted against the blaze of the setting sun, the red glow lending a strange, almost mystical quality to the moment.

Ten minutes had passed since our first sighting of the animal, and in that time we counted five or six blows. The whale was logging — lying still at the surface, almost as if asleep or in deep rest. Whalemen believed sperm whales blew once for every minute they had remained submerged on the previous dive. This whale may have respirated numerous times before we sighted it, so we had no way of telling how long it would remain on the surface. The sun was now well below the horizon, and we were losing light rapidly.

Then, with a sudden prominent arch of its wrinkled dorsal hump, the whale lifted its massive flukes and was gone on a dive that could last up to an hour. Nevertheless, everyone stayed to watch, waiting for the whale to return, until the black of night eliminated any possibility of sighting the animal a second time.

The observers filtered slowly away from the rail, almost like parishioners leaving church after a stirring service. With the coming of nightfall, the buzz of excitement died down; inside the dining area, some were playing cards, some were reading, and all seemed somewhat drowsy after an eventful day. The engines had been shut down, leaving the *Yankee Freedom* to drift on the soft southeast swell for the night.

Off the stern two crew members were jigging

for squid by the bright light of the ship's quartz lamps. I leaned over the rail and thought of the infinite variety of sea life that swam or crawled in the depths below. Of all those creatures, the whale reigns supreme in most people's minds. Over the past few decades, there has been a profound up-welling of interest in whales, the largest animals on earth. My shipmates and I had gone farther than most in our quest to see and understand these giant creatures, but many are touched by wonder about their mysterious lives.

The widespread fascination for the leviathan is a relatively recent phenomenon. For centuries we hunted whales, nearly to extinction. To the majority of 19th-century whaling captains, the idea of studying their prey would be akin to a grocer studying his grapefruit. Whales were viewed as nothing more than products, something to be harvested as efficiently as possible, with minimal damage to ships and men. Less than a decade ago, we were still killing more than 30,000 whales a year. But now the majority of hunting has stopped, and we are viewing whales with curiosity rather than greed.

Ever since the Greek philosopher Aristotle first studied whales more than 2,000 years ago, thereby becoming the first cetologist, scientists from numerous civilizations have theorized about these creatures. The most rapid growth in cetology came following World War II, as concern mounted over the decline of whale stocks and new oceano-graphic techniques were developed. Now a small but dedicated group of marine biologists, natural-ists, and environmentalists captures our imagina-tion as they encounter these giants in their own environment.

The great whales' world is so different from ours, with few common denominators between us. We know their brains are large and highly devel-oped, but do they communicate as we do? Do they have a language? A sense of history? Complex so-cial structures? These are just a few of the ques-tions facing scientists as they delve deeper into the world of whales.

The answers to these questions are vitally im-portant. We live in a strange time when it is no longer enough to ignore certain species to guaran-tee their survival. Instead, scientists and whale lovers must take an active role — directly, as when whales are stranded onshore or trapped in fishing nets, and indirectly, by learning enough about them to be able to press for preservation of crucial habitats and the final elimination of all commercial whaling.

Our relationship with these animals is no longer bloody, but it is still complex, and our en-counters have grown more frequent as we unravel the threads of their lives. In this book, we'll see whales through the eyes of those who know them best: scientists, naturalists, and underwater pho-tographers and cinematographers. Perhaps through sharing their adventures and theories, as well as the history and lore of the creatures they study, we'll come to understand how whales have so thoroughly captured the imagination of the world.

— Tim Dietz

TWO TYPES OF WHALES

All whales belong to one of two major groups: Odontoceti, or toothed whales (from the Greek words for tooth and whale), and Mysticeti, or baleen whales (from the Greek words for moustache and whale).

Toothed whales are characterized by their single external nostril, or blowhole, and of course, by their teeth, which they use to grasp prey such as squid, fish, and shrimp. Most whales swallow their food whole, so the teeth are not used for chewing. The 66 species of toothed whales also have sonar ability, which provides them with an accurate "image" of their environment, even in dark or brackish water.

The 10 species of baleen whales often are referred to as filter feeders, simply because they use their mouths to filter small schooling fish, krill, and plankton from the water. Instead of teeth, all Mysticetes have baleen plates composed of keratin, the same substance as human fingernails. Baleen grows from the whale's upper gum in hundreds of individual plates spaced about one-quarter of an inch apart. Each plate has a smooth edge facing outward and a bristly edge facing in. This allows water to pass through the feeding whale's partially closed mouth, while fish or plankton are trapped on the inside mat of the baleen. Because they feed on organisms that live near the surface, baleen whales have adapted well to life in the nutrient-rich waters near shore.

A toothed whale, the killer whale.

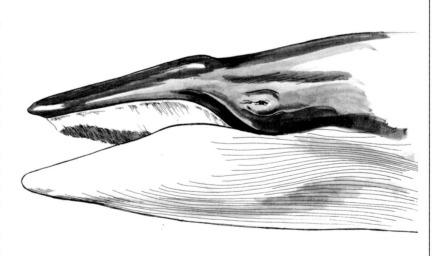

A baleen whale, the minke.

The Seekers

There is no earthly way of finding out pre-
cisely what the whale really looks like. And
the only mode in which you can derive even
a tolerable idea of his living contour, is by
going a whaling yourself; but by so doing,
you run no small risk of being eternally stove
and sunk by him. Wherefore, it seems to me
you had best not be too fastidious in your
curiosity touching this Leviathan.
– Herman Melville, *Moby Dick*

When Melville wrote these words in the mid-
19th century, he could not have envisioned the
spectacular advances that have been made in the
study of whales. We have since developed the necessary tools to penetrate the liquid world that covers most of our planet and to discover what these
creatures really look like beneath the indigo sea.

The invention of scuba gear in 1943 allowed
people to survive in an environment once forbid-
den to frail, air-breathing humans. Sophisticated,
portable camera equipment enables us to return
with images that would have astounded even as
creative and imaginative a man as Melville.

But equipment is only part of what's needed to
strip away the misconceptions about whales and
their behavior. In recent decades, bold adventurers
have traveled around the world, above and below
the surface of the sea, trying to learn more about
whales. In this section, we'll meet five such people:
Richard Sears and Mike Williamson, who brave icy
waters to study blue whales, the world's largest
creatures; Deborah Glockner-Ferrari, who was one
of the first researchers to make major discoveries
by actually swimming with whales; Hal Whitehead, who spent years at sea on the trail of the
sperm whale; and Chuck Nicklin, an underwater
cinematographer whose images of whales in mo-
tion taught the vast majority of us who will never
swim with whales what it's like to be a few feet
from a living creature the size of a tractor-trailer.

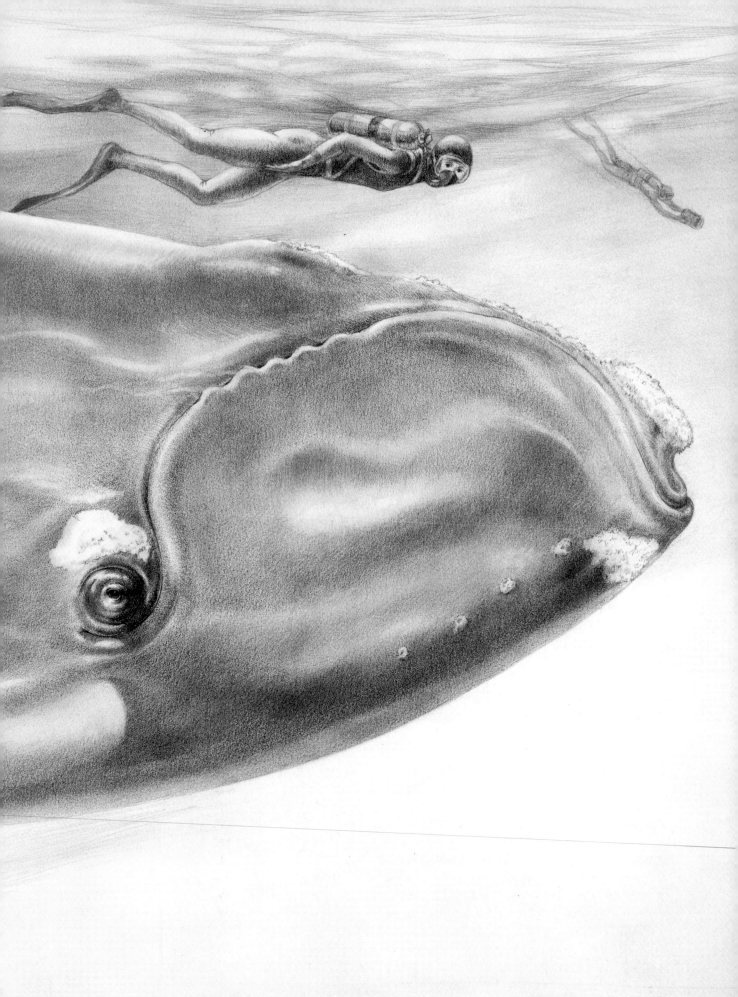

GUERRILLAS OF THE NORTH

It was a blustery cold evening, typical of February in Maine, when Richard Sears and Mike Williamson of the Mingan Island Cetacean Study (MICS), a Massachusetts-based whale research group, stopped by for a visit. I'd known both for several years, and I had invited them to my Kennebunk home to spend an evening rehashing old whale stories and hearing about their fascinating work with whales.

As founder and executive director of MICS, the 34-year-old Sears spends much of his time hustling for bits and pieces of funding to finance the group's research, which takes place primarily on the north shore of the Gulf of St. Lawrence, near the islands from which the group takes its name. Williamson, 39, is the statistics man, the "number cruncher" as he calls himself, who catalogs and interprets the data.

MICS was the first research group in the world to focus on blue whales, the largest animals ever to exist on earth. Since the study began in 1979, the MICS scientists have become widely known for their tenacity while working in a harsh environment lashed by fog, rain, and blizzards. One scientist dubbed them the "guerrillas of the north." After a review of their methods, the reason becomes clear.

In the gulf their study is limited to a three-month period in late summer and early fall, when the whales are concentrated in the area. Despite the season, the weather rarely is warm or the icy sea calm. The standard gear for a day of whale watching includes bright orange insulated survival suits and 15-foot inflatable boats in which they bound over the choppy sea, often at breakneck speeds, to keep up with their subjects, some of which grow to well over 80 feet in length.

Since both the Gulf of St. Lawrence and the Sea of Cortez in California are favored by blue whales (the former in summer, the latter in winter),

The spectacular breach of a humpback whale awes even the most seasoned researcher.

the MICS crew shuttles across the country to study the animals in each location. MICS takes every available opportunity for study because blue whale stocks have been decimated dramatically by whaling. Only a few hundred blues are believed left in the North Atlantic, while in the North Pacific population estimates range from 1,200 to 1,700 animals.

Both men also have worked with humpbacks, and as they settled by the soothing heat of my woodstove fire, I asked them whether they could point to any differences between studying blue whales and humpbacks.

"It's much more rigorous working with blue whales," Sears began in his characteristic rapid-fire style. "After several years observing humpbacks off New England, we were used to their slow tempo and the ease of identifying the animals by photographing the undersides of their flukes. Blue whales are far more massive and faster; you have to step up a gear or two just to get at them. Plus, to get an ID on the animal, the lighting has to be just right."

Unlike humpbacks, blue whales do not have fingerprintlike markings on the undersides of their flukes, so the MICS researchers photograph the distinctive mottled patterns on the backs and sides of each animal, which are clearly visible only in certain light and sea conditions. By comparing photographs, the MICS team is able to identify specific blue whales. The only drawback to the technique, which Sears pioneered and refined, is the need to get extremely close to the subjects. In 1981, when pursuing two blues for ID pictures, the two misjudged the route of one of the whales and ended up close enough to kiss its mottled hide.

"We were waiting and waiting for the second animal to surface," Sears recalled, "all the while staring at its companion, which was just in front of us. I was in the stern driving the boat, and Mike was standing up at the bow. Suddenly I hear this tremendous explosion to my left — it was like a cannon shot — and I look over and all I can see is

MICS scientists cruise among three blue whales. The sleek, powerful blues are very fast, and researchers must act quickly to identify individual animals.

this gigantic head. The whale had surfaced right next to me!"

"I was concentrating on looking through my camera lens," Williamson interrupted, "so I had a sort of tunnel vision. We were both looking off front and right, never expecting it to surface where it did. Then out of nowhere there was a powerful jolt. Sears gunned the engine, and I took a step backward to try to regain my balance. At that point I knew if I took another step back I was going to end up in the water off the stern, so I just let my legs go and dropped down into the boat. Sears was driving the boat with one hand and holding me with the other. All I remember is turning and seeing his head framed by blue whale."

Later that season, Sears's colleagues Lee Tepley and Fred Wenzel got a scare of their own. The two men were enjoying watching several finbacks lunge feeding on tremendous clouds of krill, the small, reddish, shrimplike crustaceans that are a favored whale food. Finbacks were everywhere, bursting to the surface sideways, their massive throat pleats distended as they gulped down bushels of krill. Shortly after Sears arrived for a look, all grew quiet as the finbacks dove simultaneously.

At the surface the boats drifted apart on the glassy sea as waiting gulls folded their wings and settled on the water's surface. The researchers sat tensed, knowing that several 60-foot giants were due to surface at any moment with gaping maws. "Finally one came up with its mouth wide open, heading directly toward Lee and Fred," Sears said with a laugh, obviously relishing the memory. "All I could hear was Fred yelling 'You damn motor' as he's beating on the engine trying to get it started, while Lee is yelling 'No, no!' because he's trying to film the whale."

The finback drew closer to the horrified Wen-

zel, its mouth extended to a size that could easily accommodate both boat and passengers, until it suddenly sank below the surface, missing the craft by feet. "The whale was so close," Sears chuckled, "that all Tepley got on film was a row of baleen."

Although the MICS researchers frequently use such "guerrilla" tactics to approach whales, these close encounters are usually not this frightening. The researchers point out that blue whales seem to have an uncanny sense of where the boats are at all times and try to avoid hitting them.

When Sears began his marine studies career, he didn't intend to focus on the remnant populations of blue whales, but while working on the north shore of the Gulf of St. Lawrence in 1976, he noticed several minke and blue whales in the area and dreamed of returning to undertake his own study. Before that, however, he spent three summers at a research station off the Maine coast,

learning the field research techniques that would aid him in his study of blue whales.

The first year there he met Williamson, who also had just joined the research program. The two men made a funny pair. Sears is talkative and full of laughter; he was born in Paris and sprinkles his speech with French phrases. Williamson is quieter and speaks slowly with a distinctive cracking in his low voice. But the two share a love of rugged outdoor adventure. The station on Mount Desert Rock was a rough, windswept, and often fogbound outpost, but it was one of the few places to learn about marine mammals firsthand. At times the food supply ran so low the researchers had to eat dry oats with honey. They also contended with a surly lighthouse keeper, who looked askance at the "long-hairs" watching the whales. Sears says most of his and Williamson's research skills were learned in the field. He likes to quote Roland

MICS researcher Mike Williamson is a high school biology teacher during the winter months.

Jomphe, a Mingan Island poet, who wrote, "I attend the university of the sea."

Once, when Sears was asked to row out to a supply boat packed with tourists to pick up supplies, he had an experience that may have given him empathy for whales besieged by whale-watching vessels. "As I approached the boat," he recalled, "I heard cameras going off, zing, zing, zing. I looked all over, thinking they had spotted a humpback or finback. I couldn't see a whale, so I looked back at the boat, and all the cameras were pointed at me! I hadn't shaved in a while, my hair was long, and I was wearing a big Icelandic sweater. They must have thought I was a prime example of the rugged Maine islander or something."

In 1979, with a small amount of funding from friends in marine research, Sears finally returned to the Gulf of St. Lawrence. Most of that first year was spent observing minke whales. Sears's fluent French helped him befriend local pilots, who flew him on aerial surveys in their single-engine Cherokees for a mere $20 per hour. Once airborne, Sears discovered that the greatest concentration of blue whales was near the Mingan Islands, so he decided to focus his efforts there.

One of the first things he noticed was that many blue whales lifted their flukes almost every time they dove, despite what the textbooks said. But unlike humpbacks, their flukes featured no identifiable pigmentation patterns on the underside, so this behavior was no help in developing a reliable technique to identify individuals.

After the 1979 season, California researcher Stan Minasian mentioned to Sears that he had once considered using dorsal pigmentation patterns to identify blues, although he had never done anything about it. As difficult as comparing the intricate patterns of blue-whale mottling seemed, Sears kept the idea in mind.

In 1980, MICS got a boost when it was hired by Hydro-Quebec, a Canadian power company, to do an impact study in the Mingan Island area. At the time, the company had major hydroelectric projects planned for the north shore, including the damming of two rivers near the islands. Hydro-Quebec chose MICS to help assess the potential impact of the plants on the marine mammal and marine bird populations. As a result, MICS had company-contracted planes available to study the distribution of whales along the north shore, and the team became intimately familiar with its topography.

In 1981, after two full seasons of study, the researchers finally made a breakthrough. While reviewing scores of photographs, they noticed one taken that season of an animal they had nicknamed Kits, with distinctive killer-whale scars on its flukes. Thumbing through the rest of the photos, they discovered another shot of Kits taken two years before. When they put the two photos together, they realized the pigmentation patterns on the animal's sides and back hadn't changed, giving them the first proof that blue whales could be identified by these patterns.

Using this ID technique, the MICS team has since discovered that several blues return to the same feeding area in consecutive years (Kits has been sighted five years in a row) and that many of them travel to different feeding areas during the

Richard Sears, founder of the Mingan Island Cetacean Study (MICS).

This blue whale's back shows the distinctive mottling that helps researchers identify individuals.

On a clear, calm day, a breaching humpback can be seen and heard from several miles away.

same season, sometimes swimming 300 miles or more to do so. To date, MICS has positively identified more than 200 blue whales, adding some real numbers to what had been only rough estimates of an endangered population.

Another protected species, the humpback, also is a seasonal visitor to Mingan Island waters. So far, MICS has identified more than 105 different humpbacks in the Gulf of St. Lawrence and proved with photographs that some of the same cetaceans also frequent the Gulf of Maine; waters off New-foundland, Bermuda, and Puerto Rico; and the Silver Banks region of the Caribbean.

Unlike blue whales, humpbacks are known to have playful dispositions, as evidenced by two seasonal "regulars" at the Mingan Islands named Helix and Chanty. "Helix is quite a character," Sears said. "In fact, we've been thinking of changing his name to Rambo, after the movie character, because he's such a macho whale."

Williamson added, "When Helix comes to the surface, he really comes to the surface — boom!

23

A blue whale's flukes break the surface as the whale prepares to sound on a rare calm day in the Gulf of St. Lawrence.

I'm waiting for next year when a flipper with biceps comes up and starts flipper slapping."

"On our first day out a year or so ago," Sears continued, "we met up with Helix and Chanty and decided to shut the motor off and watch them for a while. After about fifteen minutes, Helix slowly approached our boat and lined up his flukes off the stern so that we were looking right at the underside of the tail. I swear he just lined up, got set, and fired a cannon shot of water with his flukes right down the length of the boat. It splashed everyone. Luckily, I had a few guests in front of me to absorb the shot," he said, laughing.

According to Sears, Helix seems to be very protective of Chanty, whom the MICS researchers believe to be a female. Late in the 1985 season, the team was on the receiving end of a bizarre protective display from the male, which they nicknamed the belly bounce.

"We had both inflatables out in October when we ran into Helix and Chanty," Sears said. "Immediately Helix approached Fred's boat and lifted his flukes out of the water, way up in the air until they were towering over the boat. He could easily have just dropped them into the boat and destroyed everything if he had wanted to — he's always displaying. As he's doing this, my boat is drifting off to the side of Fred's boat, the motor just barely idling. Suddenly, Chanty surfaced next to us, so we knew Helix wouldn't be far behind. We tried to back off a bit, but then I looked down, and all I could see were a whale's ventral pleats under our boat."

"Over here I saw a flipper," he said, gesturing to the right. "Then over there a portion of his fluke. And there we were, right on top of his stomach! He had surfaced upside down below us, and we were sitting right on his belly!"

As Sears told the story, he imitated the whale bouncing the boat on its stomach. "I was definitely a little nervous, since we were a good ten miles from shore," he continued. "He could have easily done us in. But then I thought, 'Well, here goes Helix!' and I realized that he was just displaying as usual. Humpbacks do similar things to the larger whale-watching boats, but in the inflatable the effect is a little more dramatic, to say the least."

After a few moments of the belly bounce, the clowning humpback swam off with his partner, leaving the researchers with a fitting, albeit frightening, grand finale to the season.

As with many researchers who choose to study whales, Sears and Williamson are drawn to the task not only out of concern for whales but also because of the challenge, the unpredictability, and the complexity of the subject. Just when they think they've recognized a pattern of behavior, the whales tend to surprise them. As a result, studies need to be long-term. For MICS, thousands of questions still must be answered. Why don't they see more calves in the Gulf of St. Lawrence? Why do the blues there have so many more scars on their heads and dorsal sides than those in Baja? Where do they breed and calve? Like detectives on a trail strewn with bits of clues, the MICS team pursues the answers to these and other questions. Unless they can find some answers, the continued existence of blue whales can never be fully ensured.

"We're just getting to the point now where we're getting enough data to really start analyzing it," Williamson pointed out. "You go out and gather as much data as you can and try to put it together in a logical manner that's consistent. It's just a matter of developing the right field techniques and spending the time."

By now the evening had grown late, and the two men had a long drive back to Massachusetts. Since Sears had to get up early to depart for his midwinter research trip to Mexico, we decided to call it a night. A bitterly cold wind blasted through the open door as I waved goodbye to them, and I thought of the balmy tropical breezes Sears would be feeling for the next month or two. Somehow despite the dangers and the hustle for funding, the life of a blue-whale researcher didn't seem so tough after all. ☐

THE ENCOUNTER

You seldom hear a cetologist describe a whale as friendly or mean. Scientists distrust anthropomorphism because granting human characteristics to whales or other animals threatens the rigid process of inquiry on which scientific discoveries are based. Instead, they try to understand why an animal behaves in ways we consider human. Cetologist Rich Sears says simply, "It's a sin in the scientific community to anthropomorphize."

Yet sometimes an experience with animals will cause even the most cautious scientist to stop and wonder: How much *are* they like us? For Sears, that moment came with an encounter in the clear waters of the Caribbean Sea. As director of the Mingan Island Cetacean Study (MICS), Sears had swum with dolphins, photographed 90-foot blue whales from an open boat, and felt the salty spray of a finback blow, but his Caribbean experience surpassed any other.

He and a colleague, Phil Clapham, were 70 miles off the coast of the Dominican Republic in a tiny Zodiac inflatable boat. The gentle eastern trade wind had turned a bit blustery, making the water uncomfortably choppy, but when the two spotted a lone humpback, Sears put on a diving mask and snorkel and carefully leaned over the gunwale for a closer look. There, less than 5 feet away, loomed a fully grown, 45-foot, 40-ton humpback, its gigantic grayish black body hanging motionless, its enormous white pectoral fins stretched out from its sides like massive wings. It was eyeing Sears with a humbling intensity, slowly moving its head from side to side to afford each eye a full view of the human intruder.

"I didn't know quite what to do," Sears recalls. "So I slipped a little farther into the water — by now my legs were barely in the boat — and started waving my arms like a flapping bird. It just seemed the only thing to do at the time. Within moments, the humpback seemed to mimic my behavior,

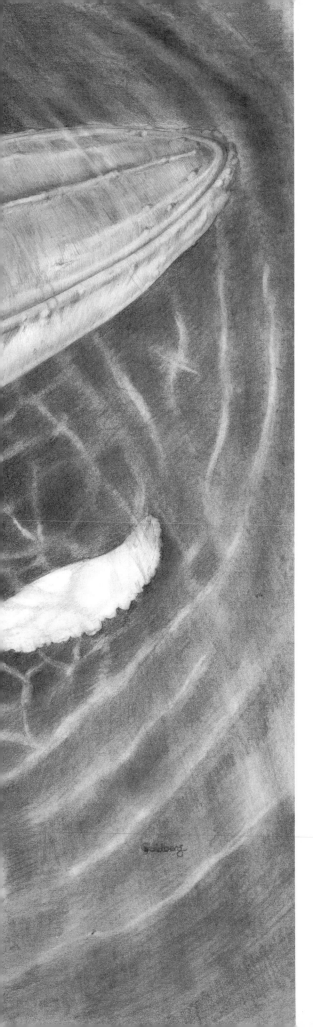

waving its huge pectoral fins as if to say, 'Hey, I can do that!'

"I couldn't believe what I was seeing! My heart was pounding. Here I was in the open ocean face to face with one of the earth's largest creatures — something that could have crushed me with one sweep of its flukes — and yet it was hovering in front of me, waving its flippers — certainly not a gesture you'd expect from a wild animal!"

Every few minutes the giant creature drifted to the surface to breathe, but it always returned to the same position, as if to keep an eye on the scientist.

"For want of anything better, I held out my arms toward the animal," Sears continues. "I was still somewhat afraid, but finally I reached as far as I could without leaving the boat entirely. I couldn't believe it when, again, she seemed to duplicate my actions by extending her pectoral fins directly toward me. Their barnacled tips were within inches of my hands. I could even feel the intense water pressure from the movement of the fins. We were reaching toward each other, almost as if we were finally crossing the void of communication between man and cetacean."

Sears was so enthralled by the situation he hardly noticed his partner tapping him on the back, yelling that it was time to get back to the main ship. When he pulled himself back up into the boat, he could see the humpback turn and swim away.

"I know for me this was the first time I saw a humpback in its full dimension, not just a dorsal fin or a fluke breaking the surface. It gives you a whole different perspective. If nothing else, encounters like that have a softening effect on what can sometimes be a cold, scientific approach. At times it made me wonder just who was doing the studying." ☐

THE BLUE WHALE

Balaenoptera musculus
("Muscle whale")

Approximate maximum length & weight: 100 feet, 150 tons.

Coloring: Blue-gray with gray-white mottling; sometimes yellow underneath, the origin of the nickname "sulphurbottom."

Food: Primarily krill but also small schooling fish.

Distribution: Small numbers in all oceans.

Estimated maximum age: 60 to 80 years.

Description: Blue whales are the largest creatures ever to exist on earth, outsizing even the largest dinosaur by many feet. The largest blue whale ever captured was 110 feet long, but since whaling has reduced the population, most adult blue whales are between 70 and 90 feet long. A full-grown adult has a heart the size of a compact car, with an aorta large enough to accommodate a crawling human. Its open mouth measures about 20 feet long, 15 feet high, and 9 feet wide. To maintain its vast bulk, an adult blue must consume at least 4,000 pounds of food per day. Blues are streamlined and fast, with 50 to 100 throat grooves from chin to navel, which allow their throats to expand when feeding. The narrow blow of a blue whale can extend up to 30 feet high.

Females, which grow larger than males, calve every 2 to 3 years after a gestation of just less than 12 months. Calves are about 25 feet long when born. (Their prenatal growth is the fastest known in the animal kingdom.) During their first several months calves require well over 100 gallons of rich milk a day, gaining weight at the astounding rate of more than 200 pounds a day.

Little is known about the lives of these agile giants. They are extremely endangered, with only scattered populations found worldwide, varying from a few hundred animals in the North Atlantic to a few thousand in the North Pacific.

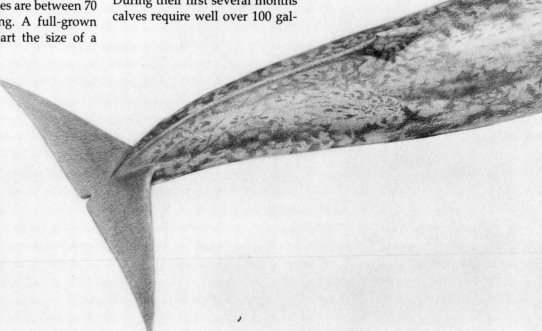

SWIMMING WITH GIANTS

It was winter, but off the coast of Hawaii the sea was warm and the breeze gentle. For Deborah Glockner-Ferrari, it was just another day at work. She slipped into the ocean from her small boat and dipped her face mask under the surface, breathing through the snorkel in her lips. Glockner-Ferrari had spotted a humpback whale nearby, and in the style that has made her famous, she went into the water for a closer look.

At first nothing seemed out of the ordinary. "I was watching the animal hang in a vertical position about thirty or forty feet below me, its head toward the surface and its flukes down," Glockner-Ferrari remembers. Then the whale began to rise toward the surface, and Glockner-Ferrari excitedly thought she might get a close view of the 35-foot animal.

"Suddenly, I realized he was going to breach right next to me. It wasn't a swift movement like you'd expect; it was more deliberate and coordinated. Then out he went!"

The humpback leaped out of the water only a few feet from Glockner-Ferrari, landing with a thunderous roar. A cloud of foam and bubbles engulfed the shocked researcher. "After I felt the force of his reentry, all I could see was a mass of bubbles. I was really frightened when I realized what had happened and just how close he had come." Fortunately, the whale had fallen back in the other direction, and Glockner-Ferrari was unharmed. Such are the risks when you choose to swim with whales, but Debbie Glockner-Ferrari's close contact with these creatures has had significant scientific results.

With only a small boat, a snorkel, and a few cameras, Glockner-Ferrari has produced insights into the behavior of humpbacks that have both surprised and delighted the scientific community.

Camera in hand, Debbie Glockner-Ferrari trails a humpback through the warm Hawaiian water.

Glockner-Ferrari has spent more than a decade researching Hawaiian humpbacks.

Each year since 1975, the 34-year-old researcher and her husband, Mark, an accomplished photographer, have returned to the waters off Maui, one of the islands in the Hawaiian chain. Her research has focused on a 20-mile stretch of water in the Auau Channel off the west coast of the island, where a significant portion of the North Pacific population of humpback whales returns each winter to breed and calve in the clear tropical waters.

Glockner-Ferrari's love of whales extends back to her childhood in Louisiana, when she accompanied her father on fishing trips to the Gulf of Mexico. There she was fascinated by the numerous dolphins she saw gamboling at the surface. She has always loved animals, and to this day, her mother says, she will even take insects outside her home rather than kill them. After graduating from college with a degree in biochemistry, she worked for a San Diego State University professor studying dolphins at Sea World; later she worked at a Mississippi oceanarium and a dolphin lab in Honolulu. While in Hawaii, she had her first experience diving with humpbacks, a day that would change her life dramatically.

In March 1975 she accompanied several other scientists involved in humpback research on a trip into the waters off Maui's west coast, just off the old whaling port of Lahaina. She remembers it as a classic Hawaiian day: beautifully sunny and calm with the verdant hills of the island glowing in the intense tropical sun. As the scientists motored farther into the Auau Channel, a humpback cow and calf approached the vessel and began circling. The channel was spectacularly clear, so Glockner-Ferrari and two other people slipped into the water for a three-dimensional look at the curious pair.

"As I first looked beneath the surface, I could see them about forty or fifty feet down," she recalls. "It was quite exciting, since it was the first time I had ever seen a humpback in its entirety. Despite their size, I didn't feel frightened or intimidated — it was a beautiful, peaceful experience."

That 10 minutes with the pair of whales and a few dives later that season inspired Glockner-Ferrari to pursue her own humpback research. The following January she began to organize her efforts. Because she lacked an advanced degree, getting the necessary federal permits to study the island's whales wasn't easy. But Glockner-Ferrari was unusually determined. Initially, she operated on a shoestring, spending days snorkeling with the whales and working evenings to make ends meet. The fame that would attract funding from major societies and conservation groups was years away.

During the first few years of her study, she focused on the mother and calf pairs that swam near shore. (Glockner-Ferrari preferred these subjects, but there was a practical motive behind the decision as well: Her nine-foot boat couldn't handle the heavier seas farther out.) As a result of working so close to the shore, Glockner-Ferrari initially ran into some problems identifying the individual animals.

The traditional humpback identification method requires getting a good look at the undersides of each animal's flukes, which have distinctive markings, much like our fingerprints. The trouble was that the whales rarely raised their flukes near shore because the water was too shallow for deep dives. To get a view of the entire animal, Glockner-Ferrari had to dive in with it. This unusual and somewhat bold research technique, which she has used ever since, soon led to her first significant discovery.

All humpbacks have large throat grooves, which allow their throats to expand when feeding, much like a pelican's pouch. These skin folds extend up to the corner of the whale's mouth, above the flipper and just below the eye. Glockner-Ferrari discovered that the pattern of these lip grooves is specific to each whale. Their number and spacing stays the same throughout the animal's life, allowing scientists to identify adults once familiar as calves.

In the first four years of her study, using traditional identification techniques as well as those she pioneered, Glockner-Ferrari identified 49 cows, 49 calves, and 23 escort whales; determined the average monthly growth rate of calves; and noted that the northward migration of the cow and calf pairs begins in March.

In addition, she developed innovative techniques for determining the sex of individual whales. Previously, scientists could sex whales only by dissection or blood tests. Through observation and photography, Glockner-Ferrari noticed that males generally have prominent white dorsal ridges, which may result from scars incurred during their battles over females. She also noticed that female humpbacks have a small lobe near the base of the tail, which was easily sighted as the animal passed in

Top, *a chin-breaching humpback.* Above, *a humpback displays the characteristic hump before its dorsal fin.* Over, *a mother and calf humpback, Glockner-Ferrari's favorite subjects.*

profile. Armed with this knowledge, she eventually was able to sex 54 females and 42 males — which, in turn, led to her most dramatic discovery.

For years researchers in Hawaii had known that mother and calf pairs often were accompanied by a second adult, called the escort whale. This animal was believed to be another female, which helped to care for the calf. Glockner-Ferrari discovered that the escort was always a male, apparently following the female and waiting for a chance to mate.

The cow, calf, and escort often travel rapidly just below the surface, pursued by several other males also interested in mating. Sometimes these suitors show signs of aggression toward the escort. On one nerve-wracking occasion, Glockner-Ferrari was in the water near two large males battling over a female. One of the enraged giants torpedoed past her, not 10 feet away, and slammed into its opponent broadside. Glockner-Ferrari was

A humpback shows the patterns on its flukes, often used to identify individual whales.

lost in the resulting maelstrom of bubbles. With fighting giants all around, she had no idea how to escape. For a few terrifying seconds, she thought she would be crushed, but fortunately the battle passed her by.

What she had witnessed was what whale researchers C. Scott Baker and Louis Herman called a charge strike, a violent form of assault in which one whale butts another with its chin, sometimes even striking out with its flukes. The barnacles on the whale's chin and flukes add what they call a "brass knuckle effect," often leaving bloody cuts on the victim.

Apparently, a challenged escort whale engages in violent contact only as a last resort. Initially, it tries to block the challenger's approach to a cow by keeping the intruder to the rear. If this doesn't work, the escort may resort to head lunging, a behavior in which it explodes to the surface, engorging its throat pleats with water and air in an attempt to increase its size and frighten off the aggressor. This attempt to intimidate opponents by looking bigger is a common defensive or aggressive display among vertebrates, first noticed in other animals by Charles Darwin. Along with charge strikes and head lunging, male humpbacks may blow straight or slightly curved bubble trails in an attempt to warn or disorient their opponents.

In 1981, Glockner-Ferrari won some long-deserved recognition when she presented a paper highlighting her humpback identification and sexing techniques to a biennial gathering of marine mammal scientists from around the world. There she received an award from the Society for Marine Mammalogy for outstanding research and for best scientific presentation, opening the door to much-needed funding.

Since then, she and her husband have continued their studies, with funding from groups such as Wildlife Conservation International, Maui Whale Watchers, World Wildlife Fund–U.S., and the New York Zoological Society. As before, their work focuses on the complex social structure and distribution of Hawaiian humpbacks. They remain especially fascinated by the interactions of mothers and calves, a relationship that seems to be filled with caring, gentleness, and frequent touching.

On numerous occasions, Glockner-Ferrari herself has had the opportunity to touch calves, which tend to be quite curious and easy to approach. One time she was watching a calf at the surface while its mother rested about 50 feet below, quite visible through the light blue water. Calves usually surface every few minutes to breathe while their mothers rest far below, surfacing every 10 to 15 minutes. As Glockner-Ferrari snorkeled near the 17-foot calf, it slowly approached her, obviously fascinated by the strange, wet-suited creature. Glockner-Ferrari remained stationary as the little knob-faced humpback swam right by her. The mother seemed to sense the researcher's gentleness and did nothing — until Glockner-Ferrari reached over to touch the calf's tail as it swam past. Apparently the little cetacean wasn't expecting the contact and gave a startled jerk, which brought its mother to the surface instantaneously.

Another memorable encounter involved the calf of an especially friendly and tolerant humpback the couple has nicknamed Daisy. As Daisy loomed in the dim light of the water far below, Glockner-Ferrari photographed the calf at the surface. "I was so involved in looking at the calf through the camera that I didn't notice Daisy slowly rising beneath me," she recalls. The 40-ton behemoth surfaced right next to her, her flukes brushing gently against Glockner-Ferrari's flippers. The startled researcher turned to face a solid wall of flesh and blubber. "She could have easily lifted me up with her flukes," Glockner-Ferrari says, "but she seemed to move them deliberately to avoid hurting me. She was remarkably gentle." The protective mother casually gathered in her calf and swam off.

A humpback explodes from the water, with the cultivated fields of Hawaii in the background.

A breaching humpback once narrowly missed Glockner-Ferrari as it landed. Had it hit her, there is little chance that she'd have survived. These animals hit the water with the same impact as a 40-ton truck.

Daisy is one of the pair's favorite mothers because they have observed her with a different calf four years in a row, proving that humpbacks are able to calve annually rather than every two years as was believed. Calves are born about 14 feet long, weighing about 1,500 pounds, after a gestation of between 11 and 12 months. Since a humpback birth has never been seen, no one is sure whether the tail or the head emerges first, but once the calf is born the mother must push it to the surface to breathe, since without air in its lungs it will sink. Feeding about 40 times a day on its moth-

er's rich yogurtlike milk, the calf grows several pounds per hour.

A calf remains dependent on its mother for more than a year, and during this time a strong bond develops between the two. A calf will never leave its mother's side unless she is killed. The mother, in turn, will fight fiercely to protect her calf. Whalemen used to take advantage of this bond, finding it easy to pursue a mother and newborn because the calf slowed the pair's escape.

Recent discoveries in the field suggest that humpbacks are extremely complex creatures, capa-

humpback — they nonetheless seem to elicit the same sort of feelings."

Like many researchers who study these magnificent creatures, Glockner-Ferrari believes that her work has a certain urgency about it. Scientists believe that prior to the modern era of whaling, more than 15,000 humpbacks lived in the North Pacific. Now, despite international protection, only about 1,000 to 1,500 humpbacks survive there, and the population may not be increasing. Marine biologists are eager to uncover any evidence that may help them better understand humpbacks and therefore ensure their survival. For instance, the capability of females to calve annually, which Glockner-Ferrari discovered, may indicate a higher birthrate than previously supposed — welcome news for an endangered species.

Some of her findings are not as encouraging. In the early years of her study, 80 percent of the mother and calf pairs photographed were swimming within a quarter mile of the shore. By 1985 the number had dropped to less than 6 percent. She blames a dramatic increase in near-shore tourist activities, such as jet ski and parasail operations — and even commercial whale watches — for this decrease. Increased development of the west coast of Maui also has led to occasional clouding of the crystal clear waters of the Auau Channel, a recurring problem that could have a dramatic effect not only on the ability of the researchers to observe their subjects but also on the humpbacks' desire to return there. To solve these problems, the husband-and-wife team hopes to get a portion of the waters surrounding the Hawaiian islands designated as a critical habitat.

Indeed, although over the years Glockner-Ferrari has overcome numerous obstacles and risks to continue her study, her greatest challenge may lie ahead: convincing the government to preserve the fragile environment to which the whales return year after year to breed and calve. This task will require as much energy and determination as she has ever shown swimming with giants. □

ble of both heartwarming gentleness and bone-crunching aggression. But Glockner-Ferrari still finds her attraction to whales hard to put into words.

"There's a special peacefulness, an almost mystical quality about them," she says. "They seem so in tune with nature. Maybe my impressions have a lot to do with their environment — I've always felt that water is pleasantly stress-free. But I think it's more than that. Working with dolphins for many years, I was aware of an innate quality, a specialness, if you will, that made the animals delightfully fascinating. Although great whales are different — you can't exactly hug a

THE HUMPBACK WHALE

Megaptera novaeangliae
("Big-winged New Englander")

Approximate maximum length & weight: 50 feet, 45 tons.

Coloring: Primarily black or dark gray above, varying amounts of white ventrally and on the pectoral fins.

Food: Small schooling fish such as sand lance, mackerel, and capelin; also krill and plankton.

Distribution: All oceans.

Estimated maximum age: 60 to 90 years.

Description: Humpbacks, named for the distinctive hump in front of the dorsal fin, are the most acrobatic of the great whales. They are easily recognized by the long pectoral fins that extend one-third the length of their body. In addition, they have numerous fist-size knobs (which whalemen called stovebolts) on the snout and a portion of the lower jaw. They are slow swimmers, usually traveling between two and six miles per hour, but they are capable of exceeding 12 miles per hour when pursued.

Their blow is bushy, between 8 and 12 feet in height. When diving, they arch their backs prominently before lifting their serrated flukes, the undersides of which feature markings distinctive to each animal. They have between 14 and 24 throat grooves extending from the chin to the navel, which allow for a balloon-like expansion of the throat when feeding. They feed in northern

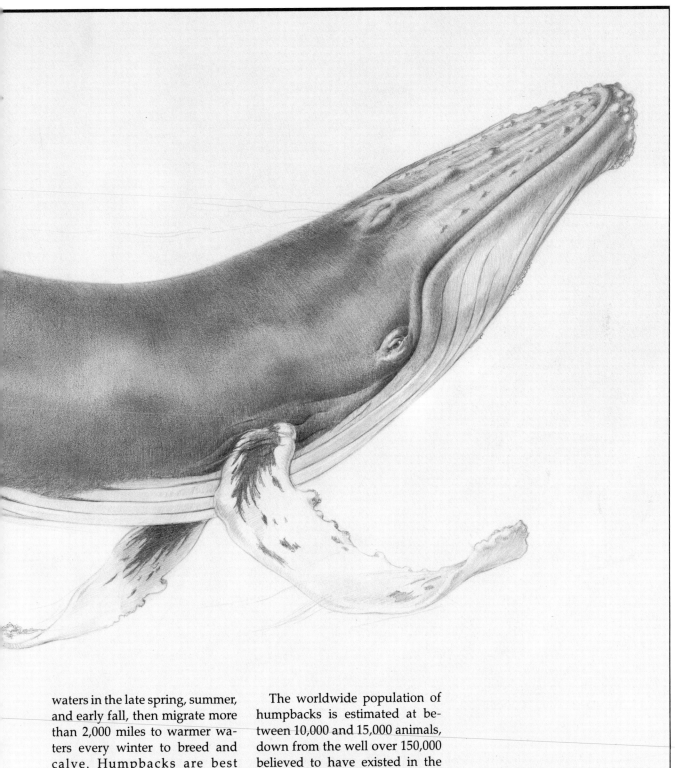

waters in the late spring, summer, and early fall, then migrate more than 2,000 miles to warmer waters every winter to breed and calve. Humpbacks are best known for their eerie songs, which are sung only by adult males, primarily in the breeding and calving grounds in temperate and tropical waters.

The worldwide population of humpbacks is estimated at between 10,000 and 15,000 animals, down from the well over 150,000 believed to have existed in the last century. There is no solid evidence that these endangered mammals are making a comeback, despite almost complete worldwide protection.

THE TULIP PROJECT

erman Melville's Captain Ahab described the great white sperm whale Moby Dick as the very essence of evil, "the gliding great demon of the seas of life." Melville, once a whaleman himself, was reflecting in his fictional masterpiece the seaman's commonly held belief that whales, particularly sperm whales, were merciless killers bent on the destruction of men and ships.

In creating his epic novel, Melville could never have known the effect his words would have on generations to come. Because his novel would be the only exposure many would ever have to the world of whales and whaling, Melville's words falsely convinced thousands of readers of the ferocity of whales.

At the same time, however, Melville also granted lasting celebrity to the sperm whale. Ask most people to draw a whale, and chances are they'll depict the square-headed, open-jawed cachalot. Nevertheless, until this decade the sperm whale remained an animal wrapped in mystery, a deep-water dweller far too difficult and distant to study. Then, in 1981, the Tulip Project was launched to set the sperm whale's reputation straight.

Organized by cetologist Hal Whitehead, the Tulip Project was one of the first studies conducted in the Indian Ocean after its establishment as an international whale sanctuary in 1979. The sanctuary was created to protect the many species of whales that inhabit those waters, and when the government of the Seychelles, a small set of islands in the western part of the Indian Ocean, originally proposed the sanctuary, it also suggested that studies of cetaceans be conducted there.

Whitehead is a native of England who learned his sailing skills during summers spent on Maine's Islesboro Island. He was just completing his Ph.D. at Cambridge University in England when he met cetologist Dr. Sidney Holt, who mentioned that the

World Wildlife Fund (WWF) had some funding available for a study of the sperm whales of the newly established Indian Ocean sanctuary. The idea intrigued the soft-spoken cetologist.

"In all my years studying whales, first as a research assistant to Dr. Roger Payne [known for his studies of right whales off Argentina and his pioneering work on the songs of humpback whales] and then on my own, sailing the coasts of New England, Newfoundland, and Greenland, I had seen sperm whales only twice," Whitehead says, with only a slight accent hinting at his birthplace. "Of all the whales, I find them by far the most fascinating because they principally live in a world we know so little about. Humpbacks, for instance, are more coastal, and it's relatively easy to

A magnificent sperm whale in the Indian Ocean clearly shows its characteristic features: the square head, underslung jaw, and massive, wrinkled body.

view much of their behavior, from feeding to breeding. Sperm whales, though, are deep-water animals, spending most of their time far below the surface. They're also animals that have few equals when it comes to concentrated might."

Despite the fact that little is known about sperm whales, their potential for awesome displays of power is well documented. When attacked, cachalots are capable of fearsome retaliation, and in some instances during the heyday of whaling, sperm whales sank entire ships. One of the better-known cases involved the large whaling ship *Essex*.

In November 1820, the *Essex* was chasing whales in the Pacific, 1,200 miles northeast of the Marquesas Islands, when it encountered a bull sperm whale that proved more than its match. First Mate Owen Chase, a survivor of the affair, later wrote that he had just escaped the flukes of one harpooned cachalot, which stove in a longboat, when he looked up and saw to his horror that an 85-foot bull sperm whale was swimming rapidly toward the *Essex* with the obvious intention of ramming the huge sailing vessel. Chase wrote: "He came down on us with full speed and struck the ship with his head, just forward of the fore-chains. The ship brought up suddenly and violently as if she had struck a rock and trembled for a few seconds like a leaf."

The whale had stove in the hull's thick timbers, and almost immediately the *Essex* started to settle into the water. The enraged whale, meanwhile, surfaced a short distance off, turned, and again headed for the stricken vessel. The second blow stove in the bow, and within 10 minutes the decks were awash. The ship stayed afloat only long enough for the crew to grab a meager supply of provisions and take to the remaining whale-boats. So began a three-month battle for survival, in which the starving whalemen resorted to cannibalism during their 4,500-mile journey across the Pacific Ocean. Only 8 members of the original crew of 20 survived the ordeal.

The Tulip Project was partially designed to determine whether such whales deserve their fearsome reputation or whether their violent behavior was simply a result of whalemen's attacks. Only a long-range study, requiring months at sea following pods of sperm whales on their far-ranging migrations, could answer such questions. Organizationally and scientifically it was a significant undertaking, and because of his education and his abilities as a sailor, Whitehead proved to be the perfect choice.

After receiving WWF approval on his proposal to use "benign" research techniques to study sperm whales — research based on observations of live animals rather than harpooned carcasses — Whitehead secured a 33-foot, diesel-powered fiberglass sailing yacht for use in the study. He chose a sailing vessel because it was quieter and steadier than a similar-size motor vessel and because less fuel was needed. Because WWF-Netherlands provided the funds for the study, Whitehead decided to name the boat Tulip, in honor of the flower symbolic of that country.

Whitehead's study centered on the waters off Sri Lanka in the northern part of the Indian Ocean, just off the tip of southern India. Although Sri Lanka had played a prominent role in the establishment of the sanctuary, Whitehead and his colleague, Jonathan Gordon, chose the area because their examination of 19th-century whaling records indicated they could expect to find many whales there.

Funding was available for a three-year period, but the Indian Ocean was too rough most of the year to conduct the study safely, so they decided to center the research year on the intermonsoonal breaks in October and November and February through April. In November 1981, after months of arduous planning, Whitehead and a crew of four set sail from Greece en route to the Suez Canal. The Tulip Project finally was underway.

It wasn't long before the upbeat mood of the crew took a battering. After passing through the canal, the tiny vessel encountered severe storms in the Red Sea, causing enough damage to force the vessel into North Yemen for repairs. The stormy indoctrination dampened the crew's spirits and offered dramatic proof of just how capricious the sea can be. Nevertheless, after a brief layover, the Tulip resumed its journey.

After arriving in the waters off Sri Lanka, the crew settled into a routine. One individual was stationed in a bosun's chair suspended at the cross-trees high above the deck. Armed with an intercom unit, this crew member would relay the location of spotted whales to an associate on deck, who recorded any observations and relayed the directions to the helmsman. Two other people took positions in the bow, taking photographs and recording data. Everyone kept an eye out for the telltale slanted blows of sperm whales.

Sperm whales can dive to depths exceeding a mile and are capable of staying submerged for more than an hour. After a lengthy dive, a sperm whale may spend more than 15 minutes at the surface, blowing every 10 to 30 seconds. Whalemen figured that sperm whales blow once for every minute they stayed below the surface on the previous dive. This predictability sometimes allowed the Tulip to approach animals within a couple of yards in order to gather vital data: photographs from above to record each animal's length; recordings of the blows to note their number and frequency; and photographs of the dorsal fin and flukes to identify individual animals. Fortunately, the old whaling records perused by Whitehead and Gordon proved quite accurate, and the *Tulip* encountered numerous pods of sperm whales.

At the surface sperm whales look like huge, wrinkled logs. The adult males, which can grow to more than 60 feet in length, dwarf the females, which reach a maximum length of just over 38 feet. Both sexes, however, feature a prominent head, which can make up more than a third of the animal's weight and more than a fourth of its length.

About 88 percent of the head's weight consists of an unusual anatomical feature located just above the upper jaw: the spermaceti organ, a complex mass of oil-filled connective tissue surrounded by layers of muscle and blubber. This organ, which whalemen called the great case, contains up to four tons of the world's finest oil. Whalemen often cut a hole in a dead whale's head large enough to descend into the case and scoop out the oil with buckets. Although the organ's exact function still remains unclear, some scientists believe the chemical composition of the oil allows the whale to control its own buoyancy by alternately cooling and heating the oil to change the liquid's density. Cetologists also believe the organ helps cachalots focus their echolocation clicks, perhaps with enough power to stun prey.

Despite the depth of their dives, sperm whales usually return to the surface within a few hundred yards of the spot from which they dove, which leads some scientists to believe that they may lie still in the dark depths, waiting for passing shoals of squid, a favorite food, until the twinkling swarms of cephalopods swim near enough. Then the whales pounce with their mighty jaws agape, ingesting hundreds of pounds of food at once.

Although the crew of the *Tulip* wasn't privy to such dramatic deep-water hunting, they gradually became familiar with the surface behavior of sperm whales. After a while it became clear that the cachalot's fearsome reputation was undeserved. In fact, the whales turned out to be shy, even timid, creatures. Veteran underwater photog-

Hal Whitehead, organizer of the Tulip Project, sights his position aboard the Tulip.

rapher Flip Nicklin, on hand to photograph a feature on the project for *National Geographic* magazine, recalls his apprehension about diving with sperm whales: "Initially I was a little worried, simply because so little was known about them. I got as much preliminary information from Hal as I could before hitting the water. On the first several dives they were somewhat skittish, and since I initially treat every creature like I would a strange dog, I didn't approach them too closely at first."

Soon Nicklin became more familiar with the cachalots, however, and he grew more relaxed in their presence. He notes that throughout the entire time he spent diving with the sperm whales, they never showed any signs of aggression. Eventually, he experienced a dramatic encounter off the coast of Colombo, Sri Lanka. "Early one evening," he recalls, "we sighted a thirty-five-foot female nearby, so I jumped in the water and swam toward her. As I moved closer, she surprised me by staying in the same spot, not moving at all. Usually they swim away before you approach too close, but this whale remained so still that I was able to swim up and pet her! Usually I concentrate on taking the photo and avoid that sort of encounter. But that was something special."

The Tulip Project not only dispelled myths about the demeanor of sperm whales but also shed light on their social structure. Because the researchers soon learned to identify individual sperm whales by their unique marks and scars (more than 200 individuals were identified), they were able to

From above, a sperm whale in the water is said to look like a wrinkled log.

study the interaction of individuals within groups. Through directional hydrophones (underwater microphones with a range of five miles), they also were able to listen to the clicks the whales emit and follow particular groups for hundreds of miles over several days. Whitehead simply adjusted the *Tulip*'s speed and course according to the direction and volume of the clicks, enabling him to track the animals around the clock at their leisurely pace of two to three knots.

These characteristic clicks, emitted by each animal about once per second, are both a form of echolocation and a method of communication. As groups of sperm whales hunt for food in the dark depths, their jumble of clicks sounds like radio static. (Whitehead likens the sound of a sperm whale's clicks to that of a creaking door.) As a whale closes in on its prey, the clicks increase in frequency until, presumably, the prey is captured, at which time the clicks stop abruptly, only to start again when the chase is resumed. Using these sound-oriented hunting techniques, sperm whales consume about 800 pounds of fish and squid each day, captured at depths of well over 1,500 feet.

Dr. William Watkins of the Woods Hole Oceanographic Institute in Massachusetts has detected distinctive patterns in the clicks unique to each animal, which he calls codas. Codas are recognizable patterns of clicks, which may represent the way sperm whales communicate with each other. Whitehead often heard codas when the whales were socializing near the surface, usually at midday. Although codas are recognizable as patterns of clicks, their meaning is far from being understood.

"This capability to track groups of whales by listening to their clicks was a tremendous asset to our research," Whitehead says. "It allowed us to gather invaluable data on the social relationships of sperm whales, an area of study of which little was previously known. At the same time, it greatly reduced the amount of time spent searching for the animals. We'd just listen in and track them down. Through the use of this method, we were privy to some unusual incidents. I recall one particularly vivid example.

"In late October of '83, we picked up a group of sperm whales near the coast of Sri Lanka. Right away we noticed a calf trailing an umbilical cord, which was really unusual because we previously thought Indian Ocean sperm whales calved around March. We stayed with the group throughout that day and night.

"The following morning dawned sunny and calm, and as we were enjoying some tea on deck around eight o'clock, a sperm whale about thirty-six feet in length surfaced not thirty yards off. The white callus on its dorsal fin suggested it probably was a female.

"Soon after surfacing she began to flex her back, raising her head and flukes simultaneously out of the water as if in great distress. Suddenly she rolled on her side with her belly facing us. Before we realized what we were seeing, there was a great gush of blood from her genital region. There, right in front of us, a ten- to twelve-foot calf was expelled at the surface."

Lindy Weilgart, a graduate student in whale acoustics at Memorial University of Newfoundland, quickly donned a mask and snorkel and slid into the water. The calf separated itself from its mother and slowly approached Weilgart, who no-

AMBERGRIS

Of all the products once procured from whales — oil for lamps and lubrication; baleen, or whalebone, for umbrellas, brooms, brushes, corsets, and collars; and meat for human and animal consumption — by far the most valuable was ambergris. Found rarely, and only in sperm whales, ambergris has been at times more valuable than gold, despite its humble origin in the intestines of sperm whales.

Ambergris is believed to form around indigestible squid beaks trapped in a whale's intestinal tract. As the whale devours thousands of pounds of squid, it digests everything except their hard beaks, which scrape the inside lining of the intestine, most likely causing a giant case of heartburn. The beaks may then act as a nucleus for a greasy, waxy substance that forms to lessen the irritation, much as a grain of sand acts as a nucleus for a pearl in an oyster. A ball of ambergris may grow to hundreds of pounds in a whale's system until it is either voided from the whale or the whale dies, perhaps even from the constipation caused by ambergris buildup.

The ancient Chinese described ambergris as Lung Yen, or "dragon's saliva," and emperors and noblemen drank ambergris concoctions to stimulate sexual desire. At other times it was used as a medicine to stimulate the heart and cure various maladies. For centuries, the sole suppliers of ambergris were beachcombers living on the tropical islands of the Indian Ocean, who found chunks of the substance washed ashore frequently enough that seagoing merchants made regular stops at the islands. Despite many creative theories — some thought it was the product of submarine volcanoes — no one had any idea where it came from.

Finally, the fishermen of Socotra, a small island south of Saudi Arabia, discovered ambergris inside sperm whales, although they thought the whale simply consumed, not created, it. Nonetheless, they pursued the giants in tiny boats in search of the valuable substance. Perhaps it was there that the current name originated; the Arabs called it *anbar*, a word found in the Coptic bible describing the "great fish" that swallowed Jonah. The name also could describe two of its many colors: *amber*, for the color it becomes after floating in the ocean, and *gris*, which is French for gray, the usual color of dry ambergris. The substance also can be black, brown, or even whitish in color. It usually emerges from the whale as a soft, black, foul-smelling mass, which upon contact with air, hardens, fades, and finally emits a pleasant, sweet odor reminiscent of seaweed.

Although ambergris was a significant item in European commerce as early as the 13th century (it is mentioned in the writings of Marco Polo), its value didn't skyrocket until the Renaissance, when ambergris was used to fix a number of perfumes. During the height of the whaling industry in the mid-19th century, whalemen always probed the intestines of a killed sperm whale in the hopes of finding an ambergris bonanza. There were even stories of entire whaling voyages being abandoned after the crew discovered a large chunk of the valuable concretion. In 1912, a near-bankrupt whaling company found the largest chunk ever — weighing 1,003 pounds — which sold for more than $60,000, saving the company.

Ambergris is still a highly prized substance, despite synthetic substitutes. Current market prices fluctuate between $100 and $150 a pound. The recent ban on sperm whaling undoubtedly will make the real thing an even rarer commodity, perhaps once again ensuring lucky beachcombers the price of gold for this strange substance, which originates deep in the bowels of a great whale.

---

ticed the afterbirth protruding from the mother. The calf approached so close that Weilgart could see the blue of its eyes.

Soon afterward, three or four adult sperm whales approached the calf and started jostling it rather violently. They squeezed the "tiny" newborn between their massive bodies, literally popping the calf up out of the water with the pressure. Some dolphins, obviously attracted by all the commotion, also gathered in the area, adding to the general confusion of the scene.

After 20 minutes or so, the adults, their curiosity satisfied, left the mother and calf alone. Once again, the newborn, its flukes still curled at both tips from birth, struggled feebly over to Weilgart, who was lingering in the water behind the *Tulip*. This time it approached her within touching distance while its mother stayed several yards away, watching.

"The calf approached our vessel and began

nuzzling the boat near the keel where the depth sounder was pinging," Whitehead says. "It may have been attracted by the sound. By this time the calf's mother had disappeared, and we began to grow worried that she had left because of our presence. Half an hour later, though, we saw the calf with an adult female, possibly its mother, and over the next ten days we saw the newborn on several occasions. Each time it looked as if it were getting stronger and more able."

The project concluded in the summer of 1984. After several seasons tracking these elusive giants, Whitehead and a rotating team of a dozen students and scientists had gathered volumes of data on the daily habits and socialization patterns of the sperm whales of that region. By analyzing this data, scientists will be able to understand further the whales' complex social relationships as well as estimate the Indian Ocean sperm whale population more accurately. In addition, the research techniques developed by the specialists aboard the *Tulip* have proved that studies of live populations of whales can yield information previously available only through the studies of slaughtered cetaceans.

"Perhaps because of Melville, sperm whales have had a reputation as being ferocious, unforgiving brutes," Whitehead notes. "Over the course of the Tulip Project, we found quite the opposite. We've swum with them and stayed with large pods for days on end, and what we discovered is that they are wonderfully gentle, tactile, seemingly intelligent, even shy animals — not at all the killers they're reputed to be."

"The Tulip Project, and studies like it, are proving there's still a great deal to be learned about the world's oceans," Whitehead concludes. "Undoubtedly, we've started to dispel some of the myths about sperm whales and at the same time taken one step toward an understanding of these magnificent creatures." □

THE SPERM WHALE

Physeter macrocephalus
("Blowing long head")

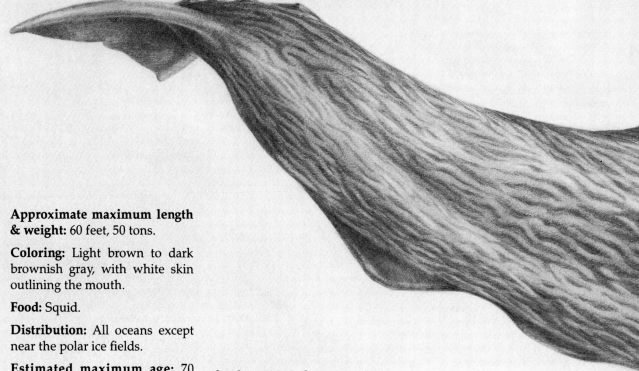

Approximate maximum length & weight: 60 feet, 50 tons.

Coloring: Light brown to dark brownish gray, with white skin outlining the mouth.

Food: Squid.

Distribution: All oceans except near the polar ice fields.

Estimated maximum age: 70 years.

Description: The sperm whale's body has a shriveled or rippled appearance, which along with the shape of its head and its unique blow (off-center, forward, and to the left), makes it easy to recognize. It also has a narrow underslung lower jaw, usually about 15 feet long on adult bulls, with about 50 large teeth. The upper jaw has no teeth. The teeth are used more for grasping than chewing; about 1 out of every 200 animals has a deformed lower jaw, which does not seem to hinder its feeding. Sperm whales are capable of submerging for more than an hour, reaching depths estimated at more than a mile.

During summer adolescent and mature males form "bachelor pods," which travel to colder waters, while females and calves form "nursing pods," which remain in temperate and tropical waters. Calves are born after a gestation of 16 months and usually are 12 to 14 feet long and weigh about a ton.

Sperm whales have the largest brains of any animals known to have lived on earth, but debate continues as to how intelligent they are. Many scientists believe they use their highly developed brains to analyze sound, creating an acoustic "picture" of their environment. Like all toothed whales, they utilize an echolocating, or sonar, ability to navigate, hunt, and possibly even communicate.

Sperm whales remain largely mysterious creatures because they are deep-water dwellers and therefore difficult to study. Despite the Yankee whaling industry of the mid-19th century, these whales are the most numerous of the great whales today, with a worldwide population estimated at about 1.5 million.

CHUCK NICKLIN'S WORLD

Chuck Nicklin is one of the world's foremost underwater cinematographers. His life reads like the original title of the five-part television series he filmed for NBC: *Ocean Quest, The Ultimate Human Adventure*. Over the many years Nicklin has been diving, he has felt the pulsating throbs of singing humpbacks in Hawaii and the Caribbean, swum the dark passages of the sunken ship *Andrea Doria*, faced uncounted species of sharks, shared the deep with pods of sperm whales in the Indian Ocean, and braved the piercing cold waters beneath the polar ice cap.

Nicklin's world encompasses all the immeasurable spaces of the earth's interlocking oceans. His work has taken him to Sri Lanka, Bermuda, Patagonia, Newfoundland, the Arctic, the Coral Sea, the Mediterranean, the North and South Atlantic, the North and South Pacific, and on and on. He has worked for scientists and Hollywood directors. Yet after all the exotic locales and the glamour of television and the movies, some of Nicklin's most memorable experiences have been with whales.

His base of operations, in the rare instances when he's home, is one of several dive shops he owns in San Diego, California, which is just south of his residence in La Jolla. In the kelp-filled waters not far from the sandy cliffs of La Jolla, Nicklin had his first encounter with a whale.

"Years ago I was lobster diving with several friends about a quarter mile offshore when we spotted a whale at the surface," he recalls. "I had always wanted to photograph a whale underwater, and I had my camera along, so we got as close as we could, fully expecting the whale to swim away. But for some reason it didn't move.

"At first I was a little hesitant to get in the water with it — in those days few people had ever

Cinematographer Chuck Nicklin aims his 312-pound movie camera at a humpback whale.

dived with whales — but I thought I could get a good shot, so I dove in."

Nicklin and his colleagues swam around the strangely subdued animal, touching and petting it and taking in the creature's massive size. They recognized it as a Bryde's whale, about 30 or 40 feet in length, a rarely sighted inhabitant of tropical and subtropical oceans.

Soon they realized why it hadn't swum away. "Because of the cloudiness of the water, it took us a few minutes to realize that the whale's flukes were caught in a gill net, which pulled the animal underwater every time it struggled," Nicklin says. "Fortunately, it wasn't too seriously entangled, although the net had cut into its blubber about six inches or so. After we realized it was trapped, it seemed like we could read all sorts of distress into the look of its huge eye — as if it were pleading for help." Their adventure had turned into a minor rescue operation, but before they set the whale free, Nicklin had a chance to get some close-up shots. These were the first of thousands of whale pictures he would take in the years ahead.

Nicklin's interest in diving and photography dates back to age 15, when he moved to San Diego from his native state of Massachusetts. At San Diego State University he majored in chemistry. Diving was still only a hobby, but in 1959 several of his friends who were graduate students at the Scripps Institute of Oceanography in La Jolla organized a company called Scientific Diving Consultants and asked Nicklin to help with a biological survey. Later, his friends left for other fields of endeavor, and Nicklin took over the company, renaming it The Diving Locker. In the 26 years since, the company has grown to a network of shops throughout San Diego.

Nicklin had found a business through which he could pursue his hobby, but his life changed forever when Conrad Limbaugh, a diving pioneer and head of educational diving at Scripps, died on a dive in France. Recognizing Nicklin's interest in diving and photography, Limbaugh's wife gave

Chuck Nicklin prepares his equipment for diving.

him her husband's sophisticated underwater movie cameras.

Using his dive shop as a base, Nicklin began venturing into the waters off his hometown to capture breathtaking images of the sea life of the Pacific. Before long, he was asked to shoot for movies and film festivals, starting with a feature film for Warner Brothers called *Chubasco*, which he filmed right off San Diego. That was more than two decades ago, and he has been at it ever since.

At 58, Nicklin looks half his age and remains extremely enthusiastic about his work. "It's a profession filled with adventure, travel, excitement, and fulfillment," he says. "I can't imagine anything offering more."

It's also a profession that has brought him some fame. On assignments around the globe, Nicklin has worked with the world's preeminent marine scientists, including Dr. Roger Payne, one of the foremost authorities on whale behavior. It was on one such assignment for *National Geographic* magazine off Argentina's remote Patagonian coast that he had one of his closest encounters with a whale.

Nicklin and his close friend and colleague Bill

Curtsinger were assigned to accompany Payne in 1971 on his first full-scale study of the southern right whales of that region. Their home for the three months of the cold Patagonian spring was the barren, windswept Peninsula Valdes, a gigantic cape enclosing two large, almost landlocked bays near the southern tip of Argentina.

Each spring hundreds of rare southern right whales — there are believed to be only about 1,500 in the world — migrate into the coastal shallows of Peninsula Valdes to mate, calve, and raise their young. Their proximity to the shore and the remoteness of the peninsula made it an excellent place for Payne to conduct his study. Nicklin's and Curtsinger's assignment was to get the best underwater images possible, despite the cloudy water and freakish winds that relentlessly batter that coast.

Since little or no diving had been done with right whales before, neither the divers nor Payne knew what to expect. Over the next several months the researchers found that despite the whales' spectacular size, they were characterized by an innate gentleness.

According to Nicklin, the only true danger came from the water's limited visibility and thus the need to get extremely close to the whales to get decent shots. On one occasion, he blundered a little too close. "We were in the water near several right whales who were courting," he recalls. "We had no idea which one was the male or which one was the female or, for that matter, how they even go about mating. All we saw was this tremendous splashing and rolling on the surface. Despite the fact that there was only about twenty feet of visibility underwater, which isn't much when you're looking at a fifty-foot whale, we decided to move in close to see what sort of shots we could get. By that time we had been at the peninsula for some time and hadn't yet gotten anything spectacular, so we were desperate."

What the divers discovered was most likely several males attempting to mate with a female,

A right whale arches its back and sounds. The dive could last a half hour or more.

which often will go to great lengths to avoid her suitors. Mating usually takes place when a female surfaces, with the male swimming upside down below her, holding his breath. To avoid this situation, the female will swim belly-up at the surface while eager suitors mill around, patiently waiting for her to run out of air. When she eventually rolls over for a breath of air, the males quickly dive, shoving and jostling to get in the proper position for mating. The resultant activity creates quite a fracas at the surface.

Nicklin continues: "As we were making our approach, I was suddenly enveloped in this tremendous swirl of bubbles and froth, and before I knew it, I was looking at the gigantic, callused face of a right whale bearing down on me. There wasn't time to react: I found myself lifted up and rolling across the top of the whale's head. Seconds later I was left behind in a pile of bubbles, muttering 'Wow!' to myself. It happened that fast. It wasn't an

This humpback breaches tail-first, showing off the animal's incredible gymnastic ability.

aggressive move or anything; I had just gotten in its way."

During their time there, the divers only once experienced anything they could interpret as aggressive behavior. Ironically, the incident occurred shortly after Payne had assured Curtsinger that it was safe to swim with the whales. Curtsinger found one of the behemoths swimming placidly at the surface and, recognizing an excellent photo opportunity, slipped into the water next to it. Immediately, the whale turned to face him, not three feet away, and started jerking its massive head from side to side and up and down. As Payne would later write, it was "churning and battering the shallow water into explosions of flying spray in an awesome display of raw power." As experienced a diver as Curtsinger is, the display must have been unnerving. Yet he held his ground until the whale's rage subsided, and nothing further happened.

At other times the scientists and photographers witnessed dramatic evidence of the gentleness and restraint of right whales toward humans. "Despite the bumps or nudges we received when we got too close, they always made an effort to avoid hitting us," Nicklin remembers. "They're very aware of you once they know you're there, and if we happened to be swimming directly in the path of one's pectoral fin, for example, it would slowly pull it flush against its side to avoid hitting us."

Like all whales that were hunted extensively, right whales had a reputation for violence and danger. At the time of Nicklin's work with Payne, no one had yet disproved the old beliefs. Because of an extraordinary encounter his wife, Katy, had had with one of the giants the year before, however, Payne suspected the whales' reputation was undeserved.

She and an Argentine diver, Adalberto Sosa, had been out in a skiff when a single animal slowly approached and circled the craft, almost touching it with its head. Turning its flukes toward the skiff,

A spyhopping humpback examines a whale-watching boat. Scientists believe coastal whales may have begun spyhopping to navigate by landmarks on shore. Over, a mother, calf, and escort humpback near Hawaii.

it swished them rapidly from side to side. Then it slid its tail beneath the stern of the boat and slowly lifted the entire craft six inches out of the water, holding its captives aloft for a tension-ridden moment before gently letting them down.

More fascinated than concerned, the two passengers made no effort to move the skiff, and twice again the whale gently lifted the entire boat with its flukes, being careful to avoid tipping the tiny craft. Since two whales with calves swam nearby, Payne and Sosa figured the whale might have been demonstrating direct, though mild, threat behavior. They decided it was best to leave.

It doesn't take much imagination to realize what could happen should a whale such as this one decide to attack a researcher who gets too close, but fortunately, as Nicklin points out, whales seem to make every effort to avoid confrontation. "I've had the opportunity to dive with just about every type of great whale, from humpbacks to sperm whales, and never had anything serious

happen," he notes. "Individual whales, like people, are different. Some are curious, others don't seem the least bit interested. But I've never seen one that deliberately posed a threat to any diver."

"The newer generation of humpbacks seems much easier to approach than the older adults," Nicklin says. "Since whale watching off Lahaina (Hawaii) has become so popular, the younger animals have essentially grown up with the industry and are used to being approached. Sometimes they even seek out the whale-watching boats."

It was in Hawaii that Nicklin became the first to film a singing humpback. On March 10, 1979, while filming *Nomads of the Deep*, Nicklin and his son Flip were off the west coast of the island Maui when they heard the boat radio crackle with the excited voice of biologist Jim Darling, a veteran humpback observer. He had something he wanted the Nicklins to film as soon as possible.

Darling and his assistants had discovered a singing humpback directly below their boat. Its

song was resonating through the fiberglass hull at "about the level of a stereo with the volume cranked up." They had noticed a humpback dive in a "peculiar twisting manner," and when they drove the boat into its "footprint" — the smooth circular upwelling of water left behind by the fluke — the song began blasting through the hull of their small boat.

Immediately, Darling donned his face mask and slid over the gunwale to investigate. There, 50 feet down, hanging head-down at a 45-degree angle, in what is now recognized as the classic singing posture, was the humpback they'd seen dive moments before. It was the first time anyone had ever seen a humpback in the act of singing, and Darling wanted to make sure Nicklin got it on film.

When Nicklin arrived on the scene, he slid his 312-pound movie camera over the stern and, with Flip shooting stills, descended to within a few feet of the singer, catching the unforgettable moment on film.

"The water that day was beautifully clear," he recalls. "There was hardly any movement, only the throbbing of his song, which felt like I was standing next to a bass drum. It makes your chest sort of vibrate. It was quite an impressive experience."

Since he first experienced the haunting melody of that whale's song at close range, Nicklin has had additional opportunities to film humpbacks in tropical waters, most recently capturing a "singer" on film in the pristine waters of the Caribbean's Silver Banks; the footage later appeared on the show *Ocean Quest*.

As exciting as Nicklin's job seems, a lot of hard work and frustration go along with it. Since his subjects are wild sea creatures, they don't always cooperate, and often it's necessary to return to an area time and time again before getting just the right shots. Usually several hours of footage are required to get minutes of finished film.

The humpback Cat's Paw sometimes feeds by submerging with mouth open to swallow small fish.

Nevertheless, beneath the ocean, Nicklin says he feels a certain freedom, an independence of spirit, which is heightened by his adventures with leviathans. Yet despite his many exciting encounters with whales, Nicklin holds no mystical feeling for them. "I don't believe they're trying to 'talk' with me or anything like that," he says. "They're simply magnificent animals, which by their presence remind you of the awesome power of nature. It's hard to beat the rush you get when filming whales underwater. I think one of the most beautiful sights in the world is a humpback gliding in the deep blue with its huge pectoral fins extended like a bird. Let's face it, whales and sharks are what keep underwater photographers busy — they're amazing creatures."

The name Nicklin will be associated with ocean adventure long after he has decided to retire to La Jolla and pursue his hobby of raising orchids. Chuck Nicklin is very close to his two sons, and they have followed in his tracks. Terry, who has traveled extensively with his father, runs the dive shop business, and Flip is becoming internationally known as an underwater photographer; he has already shot several exciting spreads for *National Geographic* magazine.

Diving with his two sons, Nicklin says, has provided him with some of his most thrilling moments with whales. Recently, far out in the Indian Ocean, as Nicklin stared intently through his camera lens at an elusive group of five sperm whales, he suddenly saw his two sons swimming fearlessly among the intimidating giants. They were engrossed in capturing their own visions of the ocean's glory. Like father, like sons. □

Lost Leviathans

One of the more baffling mysteries yet to be explained by cetologists is the recurring phenomenon of whale strandings. For as long as people have been writing history, cetaceans have been running aground on beaches and trapping themselves in harbors and estuaries.

Aristotle, writing in his treatise *Historia Animalium* more than 2,000 years ago, mentioned whale strandings on the shores of the Mediterranean Sea, noting, "It is not known for what reason they run themselves aground on dry land."

Today we are not much closer to a satisfactory explanation for this bizarre habit, which usually results in the death of whales. The frequency of such incidents may be increasing, too, as manmade structures block rivers, bays, and estuaries, changing the near-shore environment and disorienting whales. In addition, increased commercial fishing makes it more likely that whales will become entangled in fishing gear.

Ironically, these episodes provide the closest encounters most people will ever have with whales. When a whale such as Humphrey the Humpback (discussed in a later chapter) swims within easy sight of shore and stays there for weeks, millions of people who otherwise might never have seen a whale get a close view either in person or on the nightly television news. Because of the awareness they create and the information they present to scientists, the strandings have some benefit. But that doesn't mean we don't try to prevent them. In this section, we'll read about whales that became celebrities because of their trips near shore and about the people who helped to save them.

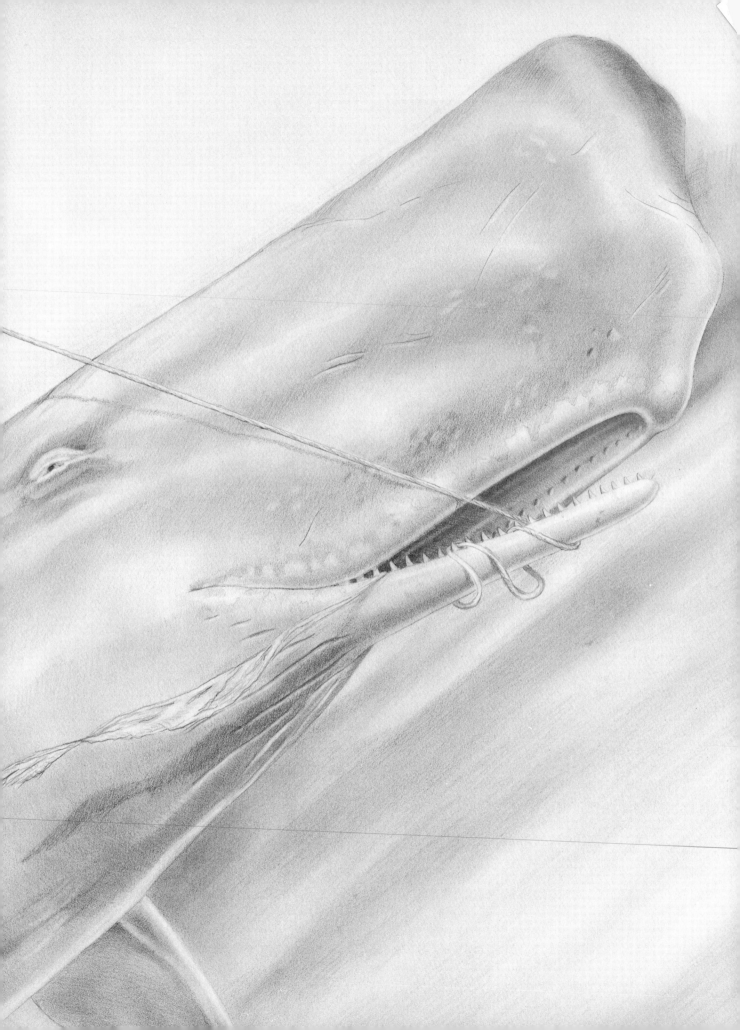

STRANDED!

Rescuers attempt to tow a stranded finback off the beach at Groton Long Point, Connecticut.

On a cold morning in January 1976, 13-year-old Shonah Smyth peered out her bedroom window at the beach in Groton Long Point, Connecticut, and saw what she thought was a huge log floating just offshore. When she saw water spurt out of the "log," she knew she was looking at a gigantic whale that had worked its way inshore from Long Island Sound. As she and her sisters sprinted down to the site, their father called the police, who in turn called specialists at the nearby Mystic Marinelife Aquarium. Within minutes, two aquarium employees were on the scene, braving the icy waters to drape blankets over the 44-foot finback to keep its delicate skin from drying and cracking.

When a 42-foot lobster boat, the *Nancy and Kim*, arrived to help out, the men fixed a rough sling around the cetacean and towed it out to open water, where they hoped it would swim away peacefully. But a few minutes later the whale returned to the same beach, lying feebly in the shallows, the surf pounding against its grayish brown rubbery skin.

By late morning, buses full of schoolchildren had begun to arrive to view the whale. Despite the bitterly cold January wind, a growing crowd gathered to see the amazing spectacle of a living whale so close by.

At first there was some confusion as to who was responsible for the animal. Connecticut had just designated one whale species as the state animal, yet marine mammals were protected under federal law. As the debate continued, Coast Guard personnel and private volunteers continued trying to tow the whale out to sea. Police officers armed with loudspeakers yelled for spectators to stand back as the boat engines roared and frozen hemp lines strained against the animal's enormous weight. The poor leviathan lay immobile, bleeding from cuts made by the sharp rocks of the beach; occasionally it lifted its head to expel a weakened bushy blow skyward.

Finally, just before noon, the whale lifted its flukes feebly one more time, then died. A hush settled over the previously noisy and jubilant crowd. The carnival atmosphere gave way to quiet, as the spectators drifted away, finally feeling the cold bite of the day's air.

A Coast Guard boat, with the aid of a private vessel, finally succeeded in towing the dead animal off the beach. The finback was taken to the Noank shipyard, where a crane normally used for yachts lifted the gigantic body out of the water and deposited it ingloriously in the parking lot. Federal officials decided to haul it to a National Wildlife Refuge in Rhode Island, where scientists would undertake an autopsy to determine the cause of its death.

The following morning, after one flatbed truck buckled under the animal's enormous weight, the finback was loaded onto another 45-foot flatbed to begin its final journey. The bizarre caravan, complete with a police escort, wound its way through the streets and towns along the way, causing schools to empty and traffic to stop as the carcass headed for its final resting place, a frozen meadow within sight of the aquatic world it had once called home. The autopsy revealed a kidney infested with roundworms, and lungs showing signs of massive pneumonia. Clearly, the animal had known it was dying.

As in so many other stranding cases, we may end up knowing the physical reasons why these magnificent animals die, but we are left in the dark

The dead finback was trucked to a seaside meadow for an autopsy. Doctors learned that the whale was severely ill, but why did it come ashore to die?

as to why they choose to come ashore to do so. Is it some hidden instinct that calls when death is near or an appeal for help in a time of desperation? As yet, the answer remains hidden.

Few places on earth have hosted more whale strandings than Cape Cod, that jagged hook of Massachusetts that juts far out into the Atlantic Ocean. In fact, when a party of Pilgrims led by Myles Standish first reconnoitered Wellfleet Bay on the Cape, days after the landing of the *Mayflower*, they found a dozen Indians on the sandy beach "busie about a blacke thing." When the Indians spotted the Pilgrims in their boat, they fled into the nearby brush. Once close, the Pilgrims saw that the Indians had been butchering one of several pilot whales, also known as grampus or blackfish, that had washed ashore. There were so many dead cetaceans on the beach that the Pilgrims named the harbor Grampus Bay.

When Henry David Thoreau visited the Cape in the mid-19th century, he witnessed such a stranding, later writing in his journal, "Looking up and down the shore, I could see about a mile south some large black masses on the sand which I knew must be blackfish." In a single mass stranding in the 1930s, more than 1,000 pilot whales covered more than 20 miles of beach on the Cape, from the town of Wellfleet in the north to Dennis in the south.

Each time the scenario is similar. First a few animals come ashore, then scores of others. In November 1982, for example, residents of the town of Brewster pushed two pilot whales off their beach but quickly reported seeing dozens of others milling offshore. The following morning more than 65 pilot whales washed ashore at the Audubon Sanctuary on Wellfleet Bay. Two years later, practically to the month, 94 pilot whales beached in nearby Eastham.

The sight of a mass pilot whale stranding

would bring a rush of pity to even the coldest heart. Their sleek black bodies lie strewn about the beach, left high and dry like flotsam in a receding tide. The occasional high-pitched squeal of their distress calls mixes with the labored blows of the dying mammals. Out of water, their buoyancy lost, they die crushed by their own weight, cooking within from the buildup of body heat trapped by their thick blubber. The few animals that rescuers succeed in pulling back into the water refuse to stay there, choosing instead to swim back to their doom on dry land, despite a seemingly healthy appearance.

Why? What causes whales to drive themselves ashore in what appears to be mass suicide? Is there a logical reason for this strange behavior?

For years scientists have been struggling with the answers to these questions, but to date all they've been able to come up with is theories. Many feel mass strandings occur when an animal leading a pod becomes ill and swims ashore, drawing all its followers to their doom. Others theorize that a leader makes a mistake and gets its pod caught in a rapidly receding tide from which they are unable to escape. The problem with both these theories is that the animals pulled back into the safety of open waters willingly return to shore. They appear to be uninterested in escape.

One belief, now discredited, is that whales, which are descended from ancient land animals, are trying to return to the land they once forsook. At the outset this may seem like a logical explanation. But why, millions of years later, would they return to land? Granted, as air breathers, the logical spot for ailing whales to go would be somewhere where they could keep their blowholes above water with minimum effort. Yet all whales eventually die from drowning after becoming too old or ill to surface for air, but comparatively few come ashore to do so. And such a theory doesn't explain why many of those stranded are otherwise healthy whales.

Many stranded toothed whales have been

These stranded pilot whales may have been lured ashore by a magnetic anomaly in the earth's crust.

found to be suffering from a parasitic infection that may interfere with their ability to navigate. These nematodes, or parasitic worms, often are found in tremendous numbers in the middle ears and brains of some, but not all, stranded cetaceans. This may be why individual whales beach themselves, but it still doesn't explain a mass stranding.

The most popular stranding theory under study today involves the earth's magnetic field and the ability of whales to navigate by it. At a meeting of the American Geophysical Union in December 1984, Joseph Kirschvink, a California Institute of Technology geologist, reported his findings that live marine mammals tended to beach themselves at specific areas along the Atlantic seaboard where the strength of the earth's magnetic field is unusually low. To establish this, Kirschvink and his colleagues compared 212 known stranding sites along the Atlantic coast with the magnetic patterns of the ocean floor. They discovered that 95 percent of the strandings occurred where bands of minimum magnetic strength intersected the shoreline.

Recent behavioral experiments have shown

that some bacteria and fish, as well as birds and bees, are capable of detecting magnetic fields and may actually use this sensitivity to navigate. Such animals have sensory organs containing crystals of magnetite, an iron oxide. This same mineral has been found scattered throughout the bodies of several species of dolphins, although there is no proof they use it for navigation. Kirschvink's study states, however, that "it is clear that cetaceans possess a highly developed sensitivity to the geomagnetic field, which probably enables them to use it for guidance."

A clue to how whales would use the magnetic field lies in the geological history of the ocean floor. Current geological theory says that the earth's magnetic field has reversed numerous times over the past millions of years. As the ocean floor spreads as a result of basaltic magma welling up at the mid-ocean ridges, a record of these changes is recorded in the volcanic rocks left on the ocean bottom, in clear magnetic stripes that tend to run in a north-south direction as they spread away from the still-forming ocean ridges. These stripes may provide longitudinal reference points for creatures sensitive to magnetic fields.

If this is true, and whales are capable of navigating by the earth's magnetic fields, this may further explain why they strand en masse consistently at specific locations. Cheryl Cornwell-Huston, a researcher from Boston University's Geography Department, has studied the phenomenon on Cape Cod and notes that there is a steep magnetic variation that runs right through the middle of Cape Cod Bay. As a result, she theorizes that the pilot whales, who are used to a low magnetic field, become disoriented by the sudden magnetic change (called an anomaly) in Cape Cod Bay, and before they can reorient themselves, they blunder into the shallows off Eastham, Brewster, and Wellfleet. This also would explain why healthy animals are involved in mass strandings.

Dr. Joseph Geraci, a noted marine mammal veterinarian from the University of Guelph in On-

tario, Canada, believes another explanation for the mass strandings lies in the group behavior of toothed whales. Understanding how whales behave as a group may explain why they die as a group, Geraci says.

A sad and dramatic example took place in the busy harbor of Portland, Maine, in October 1984 when four ailing pilot whales swam into the waters bordering that historic city. The drama began during the daylight hours of Thursday, October 18, when Edgar Lewis, a postmaster in nearby Boothbay Harbor, Maine, notified the state's Marine Patrol that four whales were milling on the surface of the cove within sight of his office. Since whales are federally protected, the Marine Patrol in turn notified Robert Gowell of the National Marine Fisheries Service in Portland. Gowell quickly conferred by phone with marine mammal stranding specialists at the New England Aquarium in Boston, who suggested trying to drive the whales from the cove to prevent them from beaching.

Throughout that afternoon, the Fisheries Service agents and Coast Guard personnel tried to drive the four whales out to sea, but the animals seemed reluctant to leave. One of them had superficial wounds on its head, flippers, and flukes, and its companions seemed to be protecting it. Finally, in late afternoon, the whales moved out of the cove, perhaps spurred by the noise of the boat engines. According to Gowell, they all seemed exhausted and were breathing rapidly. Because of their apparently weakened condition, Gowell and his colleagues feared they might come ashore again, so they kept a close watch on that section of the Maine coast.

Three days later, a fisherman working the waters off a small island near Portland reported sighting several pilot whales. Then a resident of one of the towns near the entrance to Portland Harbor called the Coast Guard to report what she thought were submarines in the water off the front of her house. Officials immediately suspected that the same four whales were making their way into the

Curious onlookers approach a lost pilot whale in Portland, Maine.

harbor of Maine's largest city.

They were right. By Sunday afternoon the four pilot whales were swimming slowly off a large ferry terminal on the city's waterfront. Gowell, with the assistance of his Fisheries Service colleague Roy Morejon, who once worked on a stranding involving 69 pilot whales, contacted several city and state agencies to make sure the whales received full protection. At the same time, Gowell placed a call to Patricia Fiorelli, supervisor of the Marine Mammal Rescue Program at the New England Aquarium, to discuss the situation. Since the whales had again chosen to come into a sheltered area, they obviously had a reason for wanting to be there, so Fiorelli and Gowell decided it would be best simply to observe them for a few days before deciding whether to attempt to drive them back out to sea.

Although pilot whales are common in the outer reaches of the Gulf of Maine, moving inshore in the fall to feed on the great schools of herring, their presence in Portland Harbor was highly unusual and immediately caused a stir at the waterfront.

By Monday, after the local media had reported the presence of the whales, thousands of interested people lined the city's aging docks to catch a glimpse of the four 15-foot mammals. Fishermen unloaded their oily catch beside nattily dressed office workers, who streamed from the city's brick and glass office towers, unwilling to miss this golden opportunity for a really close view of whales.

As the week wore on and the whales remained, the growing crowd began causing some problems for Gowell and Morejon, who were responsible for enforcing the Marine Mammal Protection Act. People were launching flotillas of canoes and kayaks to try to approach the whales. One morning, in the early light of dawn, the agents discovered three people nearing the whales in a tiny dinghy. The trio wanted to "worship" with the whales. They were asked diplomatically to leave. Another time a diver spent some time swimming with the animals before he too was asked to leave by the Marine Patrol.

Meanwhile, the animals showed no appreciable signs of change. Three of them seemed quite healthy and active, but the fourth, a female that biologists nicknamed Scarface, bore signs of extreme illness. She had visible wounds on her forehead and flippers, and her behavior was limited to hovering near the surface, moving little as the changing tide swept the whales up and down the waterfront.

A week after the group first appeared in the harbor, one of the animals disappeared, leading officials to believe it either chose to swim back out to sea on its own or was hit by a boat during a bout of pea-soup fog that had gripped the coast the day before. As the drama moved into its second week, another whale disappeared, leaving only one animal to accompany Scarface.

On Wednesday, October 31, the authorities decided it would be best to capture Scarface, pull her up on the Coast Guard station dock, and determine as best they could her condition. They hoped the last whale, which still looked quite healthy, would decide to return to the open ocean.

About this time Gowell and Morejon, who

Four pilot whales circle Portland Harbor. At lunchtime, workers from the offices in the background came to the docks to watch the sick whales.

were in the Marine Patrol boat watching the two remaining animals with Fiorelli and two specialists from Ontario, witnessed what they described as one of the most moving moments of the entire two weeks.

As their boat drifted next to Scarface, the accompanying female approached their craft and began circling on her side just below the surface, so close Morejon could clearly make out her eye staring up at the boat and its occupants. Suddenly, she started to vocalize with a sound Fiorelli later described as a cross between a squeak and a raspberry. "It seemed like she was desperately trying to communicate," Morejon recalls. "It was really quite eerie — almost as if I could sense a mood of sadness."

The following day Scarface and her companion were herded toward the Coast Guard dock, where divers slipped a noose around the tired animal to hoist her ashore with a crane. Specialists who examined the animal decided the most humane thing to do was to give her a lethal injection to save her any further misery. A later examination revealed that Scarface had been suffering from a severe bacterial infection as well as liver disease.

They estimated she would have lived only two to three days longer.

But what about the others? Since the remaining whale disappeared shortly after Scarface died, the authorities hoped all the other whales had swum out to sea. Unfortunately, such was not the case. Over the course of the next several weeks, the tale of the Portland pilot whales came to a sad conclusion. One whale reappeared and stranded on the mud flats in nearby Cumberland. The third washed ashore dead on a nearby beach. The decomposed body of the fourth whale was discovered by a diver beneath one of the large commercial fishing piers on the waterfront. They had apparently died from the same bacterial infection suffered by Scarface.

"The whole incident was purely a frustrating experience," Fiorelli recalls. "Clearly those whales were very disoriented. Pilot whales are really controlled by the herd instinct — once there's a breakdown in the social order, nothing seems to go right for them."

The story has a strange epilogue. A few weeks before the last whale was found, two Atlantic spotted dolphins, a species normally confined to tem-

THE WHALE-VIEWERS

The bodies of stranded whales, alive or dead, were not always protected by federal law. When the Massachusetts Bay settlers first arrived in the New World, right whales were so numerous that quarrels over stranded whales were common.

In the Massachusetts Bay colony the law stated that one-third of the whale's oil was the property of the Crown, one-third the property of the town, and the remainder belonged to the finder of the whale. This law was not at all popular with the colonists, who had no desire to ship oil back to England when such a need existed at home. Throughout the 17th century squabbles arose over the rights to stranded whales. An Eastham citizen even was fined one pound sterling for lying about a whale.

In an attempt to settle the chaotic situation, the Massachusetts Bay colony finally established these guidelines in March 1688, evidence of the value of stranded whales:

Furst: if aney pursons shall find a Dead whael on the streem And have the opportunity to toss herr on shoure; then ye owners to alow them twenty shillings; 2ly: if they cast hur out & secure ye blubber & bone then ye owners to pay for them it 30s (that is if ye whael ware lickly to be loast;) 3ly, if it proves a floate son not killed by men then ye Admirall to Doe thaire in as he shall please; — 4ly; that no persons shall presume to cut up any whael till she be vewed by toe persons not con-

sarned; that so ye Right owners may not be Rongged of such whael or whaels; 5ly, that no whael shall be needlessly or fouellishly lansed behind ye vitall to avoid stroy; 6ly, that each companys harping Iron & lance be Distinckly marked on ye heads & socketts with a poblick mark: to ye prevention of strife; 7ly, that if a whale or whalls be found & no Iron in them: then they that lay ye neerest claime to them by thaire strokes & ye natoral markes to haue them; 8ly, if 2 or 3 companeys lay equal claimes, then they equelly to shear.

Two years later the Cape Cod colonists adopted similar rules at the general court of the Plymouth colony, November 4, 1690, to prevent lawsuits by competing whale killers:

1. This Court doth order, that all whales killed or wounded by any man & left at sea, s^d whale killers that killed or wounded s^d whale shall presently repaire to some prudent person whome the Court shall appoint.

2. That all whales brought or cast on shore shall be viewed by the person so appointed, or his deputy, before they are cut or any way defaced after come or brought on shore, and s^d viewer shall take a particular record of the wounds of sd whale, & time & place when & where brought on shore; and his record shall be good

testimony in law, and s^d viewer shall take care for securing s^d fish for the owner.

By adoption of these rules, the colonies established the official office of whale-viewer, who was charged to examine any whale that came ashore within his jurisdiction, as well as whales reported harpooned but not captured at sea. (This was done by collecting sworn statements from fishermen.) He was expected to record all marks and wounds in detail. By doing so, it was hoped that rightful ownership of stranded or drift whales could be determined. If the claimant could not provide satisfactory proof of ownership, the whale became the property of the finder.

Two days after the adoption of these regulations, the general court appointed Mr. Skiff of Sandwich and Captain Lothrop of Barnstable "to view and inspect whales." A short time later, John Wadsworth was appointed to a similar position in the town of Duxbury.

Since the frequency of disputes over stranded or drift whales seems to have quieted somewhat in the years following the establishment of the regulations, the whale-viewers probably performed their jobs well. But the squabbles really ended with the decimation of the right whale population in Massachusetts Bay. By 1750 right whaling was all but abandoned on Cape Cod, forcing what may have been history's first whale watchers to look elsewhere for their livelihood.

As the story of the Portland pilot whales nears its sad conclusion, the lone remaining whale hovers close by while scientists examine its dying companion on the Coast Guard dock in South Portland.

perate and tropical waters, stranded on a beach just south of Portland. The two animals were helped back into the water twice before they finally disappeared. In early December the body of one of those same two dolphins, identified from photographs taken at both stranding sites, washed up on the sandy shores of East Dennis, Cape Cod. Because it was the northernmost appearance ever of a spotted dolphin, the skeleton was preserved at the Smithsonian Institution in Washington, D.C. Fiorelli theorizes that the appearance of the Portland pilot whales and the tropical dolphins may have somehow been connected. The fact that these species appeared so far out of their element all at one time seems more than a coincidence, although Fiorelli can offer no explanation for why it happened.

As recently as a few decades ago, such strandings were considered windfalls in many areas because they provided free food and oil for the residents; the stranded whales were simply butchered and processed. But since whales have become protected species, the public role has changed from that of user to that of protector. Now many of us feel that something must be done to prevent such mass deaths. Sadly, we are far from solving this mystery. □

THE PILOT WHALE

Globicephala melaena
("Globe-headed black whale")

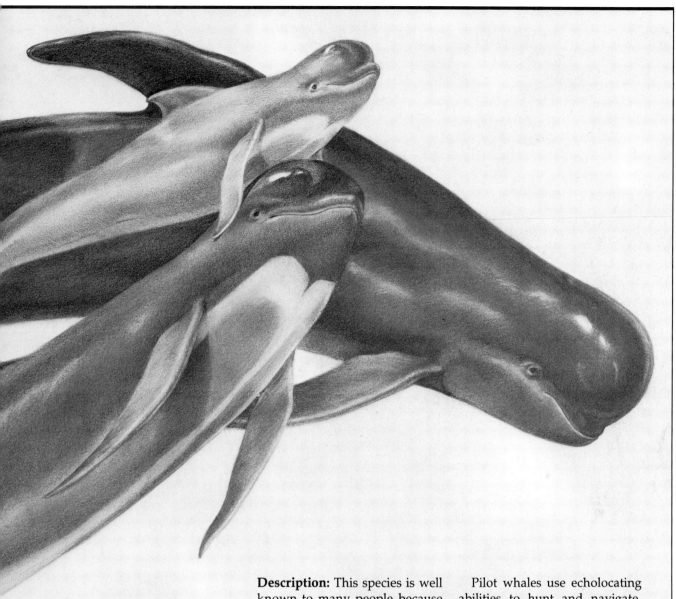

Approximate maximum length & weight: 20 feet, 7,000 pounds.

Coloring: Jet-black with white anchor-shaped patch on chin.

Food: Squid and schooling fish.

Distribution: Cold and temperate waters of the North Atlantic and Southern Hemisphere.

Estimated maximum age: 50 years.

Description: This species is well known to many people because of its tendency for mass strandings. In one such incident in the 1930s, more than 1,000 pilot whales washed ashore on the beaches of Cape Cod. Although the exact reason for this behavior is unknown, pilot whales are known to possess a strong herding instinct and often are found in concentrations of several hundred individuals. The pilot whale's bulbous forehead earned it the whaling nickname "pothead," but it is also referred to as a blackfish.

Pilot whales use echolocating abilities to hunt and navigate. They are deep divers, capable of submerging to depths beyond 2,000 feet. Because of this talent, as well as their trainability, pilot whales have been used in several U.S. Navy projects to recover small sunken pieces of military equipment.

There are two species of pilot whales: long-finned, described here, and short-finned, which inhabit the tropical waters of the Atlantic, Pacific, and Indian oceans. Pilot whales are not an endangered species.

Warriors, Kings fall short in season debuts
Sports/Page C-1

The Roches: Singing muggers
Style/Page B-1

Can 49ers kick their losing habit?
Sports/Page C-2

San Francisco Examiner

25¢   Saturday, October 26, 1985   California ★

Where's Humphrey?

Whale escapes slough, vanishes into the night

State of emergency in Cape Town as police kill 2 blacks

ASSOCIATED PRESS

JOHANNESBURG — Police today said they shot and killed two blacks in unrest near Cape Town, where the government declared a state of emergency and arrested anti-apartheid activists yesterday.

The latest deaths were included in a police report covering violent incidents and unrest from sundown yesterday until dawn. Both killings were in Cape Province, police said, but said they did not know if the victims died yesterday or today. The state of emergency took effect at midnight.

In Guguletu, a black township east of Cape Town, police said rioters threw a gasoline bomb at a truck. Police said they fired at the rioters with shotguns, killing one.

In a black area outside Beaufort West, farther inland from Cape Town and not covered by the new state of emergency, police said they shot and killed a black man in a group of people throwing gasoline bombs and rocks at security vehicles.

The proclamation yesterday of a state of emergency in the Cape Town area followed an anti-apartheid rampage through the city's fashionable white shopping district the day before, and two months of unrest in the city's black and mixed-race suburbs.

At least 60 people have been killed in recent rioting in the Cape Town region, according to news reports.

In announcing the state of emergency, Law and Order Minister Louis le Grange said: "The unrest situation in the western Cape ... has reached such proportions that the government has decided to declare a state of emergency in certain districts."

He said President P.W. Botha signed a proclamation adding Cape Town and seven surrounding towns to the 30 covered under emergency law since July 21. Areas covered previously include Johannesburg

— Please see AFRICA, A-10

Reagan will send Shultz to meet with Gorbachev

ASSOCIATED PRESS

WASHINGTON — President Reagan, described as "extremely pleased" with growing allied solidarity, is sending Secretary of State Shultz to meet with Soviet leader Mikhail Gorbachev in an attempt to narrow superpower differences before the Geneva summit.

Shultz, following a two-hour meeting with Soviet Foreign Minister Eduard A. Shevardnadze in New York yesterday, virtually ruled out the possibility that Reagan and Gorbachev would conclude an arms-control agreement at their Nov. 19-20 summit meeting.

But he said a major summit objective would be to "set out an agenda for the future, to have a sense of direction of where we think and they think this relationship should go."

With Reagan's encouragement, Shultz said he accepted a Soviet invitation to meet with Gorbachev in Moscow on Nov. 4-5.

"I would have to say there are

major differences that need to be resolved, and we hope that some of them may get resolved before the meeting in Geneva," Shultz told reporters outside the U.S. Mission to the United Nations following his breakfast meeting with Shevardnadze.

The Soviet foreign minister told reporters that "great hopes are pinned to that summit meeting by literally all peoples in the world," and that both sides were dedicated to seeking a successful outcome.

Shultz and other U.S. officials denied that Reagan had decided to make a counteroffer to Gorbachev's recent proposal for a 50 percent reduction in nuclear missiles and warheads.

But these officials left open the possibility that Reagan might decide on a U.S. response in time for Shultz to take it to Moscow. Robert C. McFarlane, the president's national security adviser, told reporters that Reagan wants to make "a timely response" to Gorbachev's

— Please see REAGAN, A-10

Humphrey the whale raises a fin before he was herded through bridge supports yesterday

Associated Press

By Dwight Chapin
OF THE EXAMINER STAFF

RIO VISTA, Solano County — Humphrey, the lost humpback whale who yesterday wriggled and flopped and finally squeezed through what could have been a fatal barrier on Shag Slough, appeared to be on his way toward the Pacific when marine biologists lost track of him in darkness last night.

At 7:30 p.m. Humphrey approached the bridge across the Sacramento River at Rio Vista — and suddenly the 45-foot, 45-ton beast was gone.

Elation of would-be rescuers — whose imaginative underwater-sound tactics to urge him oceanward appeared to be working — turned to fear that he may have doubled back and entered any of three main Sacramento River tributaries.

Two California Highway Patrol helicopters spent an hour flying low over the river with spotlights. Officials appealed to the thousands of tourists and Delta residents who have followed the whale's wandering to report any sight of him by calling (707) 374-2612.

The whale, who entered the labyrinthine Delta waterways Oct. 11, has been unable to find his way back to the ocean. If he is sighted again, whale experts plan to attach a radio transmitter to his hide, by means of a suction cup, to monitor his movements.

It was 4 p.m. when Humphrey swam clumsily oceanward between the wooden supports of the Liberty Island Bridge, six miles north of Rio Vista. The structure's tightly spaced poles had imprisoned him in a shallow slough since last week, when he somehow squirmed through.

Some observers speculated that he may have injured himself squeezing through the first time and feared going back.

For most of the day, Humphrey

— Please see WHALE, A-10

Auto body repairman to spin wheel for $2 million

By Walt Gibbs
OF THE EXAMINER STAFF

Joe McAlpin, 45, was sitting at Ike's Acme Club bar in Oakley last night making plans "to throw one hell of a party that Oakley will never forget."

The auto body repairman, who hasn't had much work lately, was informed by telephone yesterday at 11 a.m. that he has qualified as one of the potential winners of $2 million in the state's new lottery.

"I've been drinking and partying and getting down," McAlpin said an hour before the bar closed. It is in

eastern Contra Costa County. "I'm going to win that $2 million."

He is guaranteed $10,000.

"I have not come down from a natural high yet, but when I do it's going to hurt," he said, rubbing his head.

McAlpin has a wife, Barbara, two children and a 2-month-old grandchild, Heather.

Any way you figure it, he will be richer on Nov. 4, along with nine others.

That's the date of the second grand-prize California Lottery drawing, and the amounts those people can win are $10,000, $50,000, $100,000 or $2 million. Each will win

one of those four amounts, depending on the spin of the wheel.

The first drawing, Monday, has 20 qualifiers.

Qualifiers for the drawings were selected from winners of $100 prizes in the state lottery. The finalists were chosen from 6,250 winners of $100 lottery prizes.

Besides McAlpin, they were as Rosabelle Gold, of San Francisco; Jose Caballero and Robin Osar, both of San Jose; Harry Ney of Modesto; Don Sharp of Oakdale; and four Southern Californians: Rosemarie Forsyth, Oxnard; Richard Miranda, Baldwin Park; Naomi Garrison, Chino; and James Smith, Pa-

coima.

"This really is real?" wondered Mavis Sharp, 33, of Oakdale, when lottery officials called to notify her husband, Don.

"I called my husband at the office. He said, 'Somebody is playing a joke on you,' " she said.

The players were drawn by Sacramento County Board of Education member Roy Grimes, who was blindfolded as he plucked 10 sealed capsules out of a plastic drum.

Lottery officials now say at least 150 million tickets have been sold

— Please see LOTTERY, A-10

HUMPHREY'S STRANGE ODYSSEY

Sometime on Friday night, October 11, 1985, under the cover of fog-shrouded darkness, a lone humpback whale swam into the turbulent waters at the mouth of San Francisco Bay, passing silently like a prowling submarine under the blinking lights of the Golden Gate Bridge. The whale sliced through the dark waters with a silence and grace that belied its enormous bulk; occasionally it rose to blow, mixing its pufflike breath with the moaning bay foghorns.

On its southbound migration from Alaska to the warm waters of its breeding and calving grounds in Hawaii, the humpback decided for some unknown reason to vary its course to the east, into one of the most densely populated bay areas in the world. Perhaps it was following the call of a singular gene, leading it to a primordial breeding ground long gone with the coming of man. Perhaps it was drawn by an underwater signal emanating from one of the bay's military defense systems. No one knows for sure.

At midnight Peter Chorney, senior resident agent with the Law Enforcement Division of the National Marine Fisheries Service (NMFS) in nearby Santa Rosa, was startled awake by a phone call from the Coast Guard. It turned out to be routine: The officer was reporting the presence of a large whale in the bay. According to the caller, the whale was swimming in shallow water near Oakland's Outer Harbor.

There was little cause for concern, Chorney thought sleepily. Each year several whales make their way into the bay and just as easily find their way out. The Coast Guard worries about shipping; the Fisheries Service worries about curious boaters harassing the whales. Chorney requested that the Coast Guard keep an eye on the position of the whale and advise the NMFS should any enforcement problems occur. He sighed and went back to

For a time, Humphrey the lost humpback made headlines across the country.

bed, fully expecting the errant whale would be gone by morning.

Such was the sleepy introduction to what would become the world's most famous living whale. Over the next 25 days, more than a dozen state and federal agencies, media from around the world, hundreds of volunteers, and an international cast of whale specialists would draw together to save the life of what seemed to be a hopelessly disoriented humpback whale meandering through one of the world's largest landlocked harbors and its many estuaries.

October 12

Early the following morning, the 45-foot, 40-ton leviathan, which was now beginning to attract interested crowds, stranded briefly on a sandbar near the Berkeley Marina, its enormous glossy black body lying exposed to the blistering sun and the sharp beaks of sea gulls. While worried adults and delighted children pointed and shouted, the spirited animal flapped its gigantic pectoral fins, arched its mighty back, and with a thrust of its tail, bolted free of its shallow prison in a plume of mud and spray.

Now at his NMFS office, Chorney authorized three volunteer vessels to attempt to guide the animal back toward the Golden Gate Bridge and the open waters of the Pacific. Eager volunteers from the California Marine Mammal Center (CMMC) in nearby Marin County joined the Coast Guard vessels in attempting to steer the humpback in a westerly direction, much as a rancher would direct a stray bull back to the herd. The boats raced to the animal's rear and from one side to the other every time it varied from the proper course. But as it would prove repeatedly over the next several weeks, this humpback had other ideas.

The whale swam a couple of miles back toward the ocean, but in the vicinity of Angel Island, a state park not two miles from the Golden Gate Bridge, it abruptly changed its course due north toward San Pablo Bay, where it spent the remainder of the day fascinating gathering crowds of land-based spectators, most of whom had never seen a whale before.

October 13 and 14

Through much of Sunday the whale continued quietly crisscrossing the waters of San Pablo Bay. Late that afternoon, however, it started an eastward journey through the Carquinez Strait, toward the Sacramento River Delta and its maze of freshwater streams and rivers. Biologists from the NMFS and the CMMC became increasingly worried as the whale passed from salt water to fresh water, a potentially deadly change for the animal. To date, little is known about the effects of fresh water on an oceangoing mammal, but scientists theorized that the decreased salinity could cause the humpback breathing and buoyancy problems because it would need more energy to swim in water that offered less support for its massive bulk. There also was the possibility that the whale might suffer skin and eye damage from the drastic change in environment. As a result, the authorities held little hope for the animal's survival if it continued its journey into the muddy waters of the Sacramento River Delta.

On Monday morning, the CMMC called Chorney to tell him the humpback had been sighted in the vicinity of the New York Slough, almost 20 miles up the Sacramento River, well into the freshwater region. After a brief discussion with other Fisheries Service agents, Chorney authorized the CMMC to use underwater sounds to try to frighten the confused humpback back downriver toward salt water.

The plan was simple. Through underwater hydrophones dragged by small boats in front of the whale, the biologists would play recordings of killer whales, which occasionally prey on humpbacks, in an attempt to scare the animal downstream. Although there was no conclusive proof that it would work, the idea was based on the knowledge that whales are highly sound-sensitive animals, which may use sound to find their way through the trackless reaches of open ocean. By playing recordings of killer whales, they hoped to trick the humpback into thinking its path upstream was populated by the predatory mammals. Much to the chagrin of the would-be rescuers, however, the whale apparently was unfazed by the threatening sounds and continued its journey upriver toward the small town of Rio Vista, deep in the heart of the nation's largest agricultural valley.

October 15

By now word of the whale's presence was spreading, and hundreds of tourists were gathering to watch the bizarre spectacle of a whale swimming peacefully in a freshwater river banked by cornfields and farms. California Highways 160 and 12 jammed with traffic as farmers and ranchers turned whale watchers flocked to the riverbank. For Chorney, protecting the whale from curious boaters was becoming a problem. To clear the crowded area around the whale, the Fisheries Service issued a warning that the animal was federally protected and that any visible harassment was punishable by fines of up to $20,000.

Hundreds of miles to the south in Long Beach, Fisheries Service biologist Sheridan Stone, who had just returned from a business trip to Colorado, was receiving regular updates from Chorney on the whale's movements. As a wildlife biologist and regional coordinator of the California Marine Mammal Stranding Network, he soon would be drawn beyond casual contact with the drama, which was gaining media momentum with every mile the whale swam inland.

Meanwhile, the humpback — now nicknamed *E.T.* by biologists familiar with the lost movie creature — once again stranded on a sandbar, this one near Decker Island, less than four miles downriver from Rio Vista. For more than an hour it struggled to free itself, its muddy, exposed back drying in the sun. But while hurried plans were being made to spray the whale with water to

To the bewilderment of scientists, Humphrey swam more than 75 miles up the Sacramento River, spending nearly a month away from his ocean home.

keep its skin from peeling, the feisty cetacean finally wriggled free, much to the relief of the huge crowd trampling the riverbank, which began to cheer its every movement. Instead of heading downstream, however, as it appeared to be before stranding, the confused humpback started inland again toward Rio Vista.

In the short time since the whale had appeared, Rio Vista had become a tourist mecca of sorts. One eatery in town, The Point Restaurant, offered a luncheon special named the Humpback Open Face Seafood Sandwich as well as a dinner special called Swordfish à la Humphrey. That dish may have been the origin of the nickname by which the country soon knew the lost humpback — Humphrey — an appropriate appellation because scientists believed it was a male, judging by the scars it displayed.

As evening fell, Humphrey swam north beneath the Rio Vista bridge and turned left, avoiding the Sacramento Deep Water Ship Channel, which carries oceangoing vessels to the port of Sacramento. He spent the night at the mouth of nearby Cache Slough, swimming lazily nearly a third of the way across California, a full 70 miles inland from the Golden Gate Bridge.

October 16 through October 18

Early Wednesday morning, the Fisheries Service agents went aloft in a Coast Guard helicopter to locate Humphrey, who they easily spotted swimming just north of Rio Vista. For the next several minutes, in a series of low passes and sharp turns, they tried using the noise of the helicopter to direct the cetacean downstream, with no success. Although humpbacks in Alaska and Hawaii are known to respond to the presence of helicopters, Humphrey paid no attention, maintaining his composure as he continued to surface and blow in his rhythmic fashion.

During the next several days Chorney organized a 24-boat flotilla of vessels from the Coast Guard, local county sheriffs' offices, and authorized volunteers, who again tried directing Humphrey toward the sea, at one point succeeding in moving him six miles downriver, only to be thwarted by his reluctance to pass back under the Rio Vista Bridge on Highway 12.

"We consulted with several engineers as to why the whale refused to pass under the bridge," Chorney recalls. "The general opinion was that the noise of the traffic as well as the sandblasting — they were repainting the bridge at the time — was

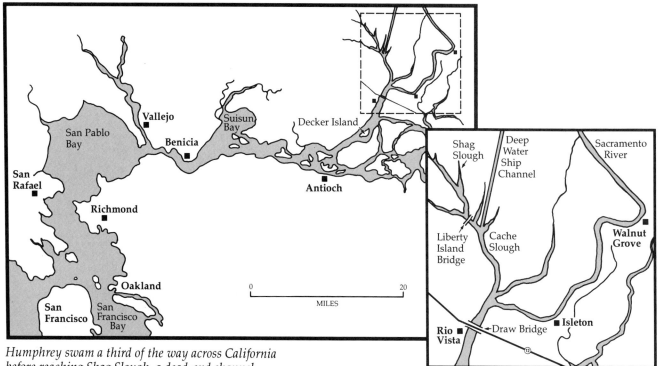

Humphrey swam a third of the way across California before reaching Shag Slough, a dead-end channel.

scaring the humpback away. So when the animal began to approach the bridge, all work was stopped." Nevertheless, Humphrey refused to swim beneath it, always timidly turning inland when he moved close to the structure.

As the level of interest in the whale escalated, everyone wanted to get into the act. Telephone lines into the various organizations and agencies involved in the rescue were jammed, as nearly 10,000 people called offering advice on how to save the beleaguered giant.

One caller suggested dropping small explosives into the river to frighten the cetacean downstream, although he didn't say who would clean up all the dead fish or cure Humphrey's hearing afterward. Another suggested dropping a trail of salt cubes to lure Humphrey back to the sea (nicknamed "The Saline Solution" by the San Francisco *Chronicle*). Numerous callers suggested recruiting a team of dolphins from the nearby Marine World/Africa USA theme park to lead Humphrey to freedom, although no one was sure who would, in turn, lead the dolphins. Parapsychologists offered to perform psychic healings on the whale's "tortured soul" by standing nearby and thinking positive thoughts. Some even suggested dropping a female humpback into the delta so the pair could

"swim in harmony to the sea."

One Sacramento woman, claiming she was "earthquake sensitive," blamed Humphrey's misguided journey on a Russian earthquake, which she said emitted high-frequency vibrations that scrambled the whale's "sonar navigation system." She suggested exposing the animal to either a magnetic pulse or a high-frequency noise, which would readjust his navigation system. In a different vein, one man who used to operate a California shore whaling station offered this solution: Harpoon the whale and process him for oil.

By the end of the first week of Humphrey's odyssey, he had become a national celebrity, with regular reports on his progress, or the lack of it, featured in daily newspapers around the country as well as on network news and talk shows. Down in the regional office of the Fisheries Service in Los Angeles, Stone was handling a torrent of inquiries from the press. "Interest in the whale was intense," he recalls. "There were more calls coming in than I could handle myself." Finally, a second biologist was brought in to help.

October 19 and 20

After several failed attempts to drive Humphrey downstream, Chorney's regional office suggested that all rescue operations be suspended until Monday, the twenty-first, when an alternative plan might be available.

Humphrey, meanwhile, had made his way even farther north, squeezing between the narrow pilings of the Liberty Island Bridge and entering Shag Slough, a 10-foot-deep, dead-end channel less than 30 miles from the state capital, Sacramento. There he was confined to a narrow strip of fresh, muddy water less than half a mile long, bordered at one end by the pilings of the Liberty Island Bridge and at the other by shallow mud flats. He could go no farther. Yet despite this seemingly hopeless scenario, Humphrey remained extremely active, swimming in circles and occasionally rolling over on his side to slap the water's surface with his 15-foot white pectoral fins, delighting the crowds of media people and tourists on the shore, most of whom had never seen a humpback whale, much less one this close.

By now, Chorney was putting in 15- to 18-hour days ensuring the whale's safety. He patrolled the slough, warning small boat owners to maintain their distance, until eventually he found it necessary to declare the slough off-limits to private boats.

As Humphrey's weekend of rest from rescue efforts continued, Stone and his colleagues in the regional office were busy contacting whale behaviorists and marine mammal veterinarians to determine the next logical step. The experts all agreed that Humphrey was under physiological stress from prolonged exposure to fresh water and, if left on his own, probably would not find his way out. They decided it was necessary to continue trying to move the hapless cetacean.

Dr. Kenneth Norris, a noted marine mammal expert from the University of California at Santa Cruz, suggested trying a Japanese dolphin-driving technique called *oikoime* to move the whale. The technique involves the use of several water-filled pipes, each about eight feet long and two inches in diameter, which are set over the side of a boat and tapped lightly with hammers to create a pinging sound. The Japanese use oikoime to herd schools of dolphins and porpoises out of shallow water.

"Dr. Norris suggested this method simply because it was a somewhat proven technique," Stone notes. "To date, all our other attempts had failed, and although the Japanese method was known to work only with dolphins and porpoises, we decided it would be our next course of action, depending on the whale's condition."

Since the situation showed signs of persisting, and Chorney and the Coast Guard were having a difficult time dealing with both enforcement and press inquiries, Stone flew to San Francisco the next day to take some of the pressure off them. When he arrived at the slough, Stone was amazed by the general hubbub created by Humphrey's presence.

"Although we had enforcement agents keeping people back, there was still a tremendous amount of activity," he says. "There was a van already selling Humphrey T-shirts as well as TV cameras everywhere, but most of the people were very orderly — just happy to be able to observe."

Stone's first concern was with the whale, and his initial look at the delta's most famous resident was encouraging. "He looked quite normal to me," Stone says. "His breathing and surfacing looked to be within normal ranges, to the extent of what we understand to be normal for a humpback, and he seemed to be well oriented, although his skin seemed a bit lighter gray than the darker colored humpbacks I was familiar with from my observations in Antarctica. Generally, he was a good-size animal with a healthy look and vigorous movements, although, of course, he was confined within in the slough."

October 23

After watching Humphrey circle Shag Slough for several days, frustrated Fisheries Service officials decided the whale had been on his own long enough and it was time to begin driving him back to sea with the Japanese dolphin-driving method. But because of the tremendous distance involved and the clear need for additional help, it was necessary to mobilize state agencies.

With the urging of his children, State Senator John Garamendi, from the nearby town of Walnut Grove, contacted the Director of California's Office of Emergency Services (OES) to request assistance in coordinating numerous state agencies in a massive whale rescue operation. The Fisheries Service scheduled a meeting of all local, county, and state agencies that evening at the Coast Guard station in Rio Vista.

That afternoon, the Fisheries Service held a press conference to tell people that access to the whale would be highly restricted during the remainder of the rescue operation, with spectators kept at least 100 yards away, no air traffic nearer than 1,000 feet, and all automobile traffic halted within a half mile of the whale. The idea was to keep the area surrounding the animal as acoustically "clean" as possible to make sure that Humphrey wasn't confused by sounds other than the clanging pipes. During the press conference Fisheries Service agent James Lecky pointed out that "even a man pounding a Coke can flat on the shore can cause the whale to respond." In addition, Lecky said that several major highway closings were possible, including Highway 12 across the Rio Vista Bridge, once the whale swam into their vicinity.

Even though the decision had been made to proceed with the rescue effort, several whale experts disagreed about its advisability. Jim Hudnall from the Maui Whale Institute in Santa Cruz didn't think Humphrey should be forced to move because the animal hadn't yet shown any signs of distress. "I am really concerned that the authorities are going to move this whale without any real idea as to why it should be moved," he said. Other experts agreed, but for a different reason: They believed Humphrey was going to die anyway and shouldn't have to endure the additional stress

caused by the clanging pipes. Nonetheless, the Fisheries Service agents proceeded.

A command center for the operation was established at a nearby construction company; a Coast Guard cutter, the *Point Heyer*, was brought in from San Francisco; sport fisherman Jack Findleton, who was intimately familiar with the myriad estuaries of the delta, was assigned to the operation; housing for the scores of volunteers was arranged at the U.S. Army Reserve Base in Rio Vista; a group of government and private boats was readied; California Conservation Corps members were mobilized for a two-day operation; law enforcement agencies cleared the area and set up roadblocks; and standby plans for moving, tagging, and even the possible disposal of the whale were made.

Meanwhile, the center of all this attention swam placidly in the shallows of Shag Slough, little suspecting the mobilization underway on his behalf.

October 24

Throughout the two-week ordeal, theories of why Humphrey swam so far inland were bandied about. Some, like the Russian earthquake theory, probably were ridiculous. Others, like the belief that Humphrey had swum upriver in search of food, were more plausible. One of the more interesting conjectures concerned acoustics. One official theorized that Humphrey was attracted by transmissions from a U.S. Navy high-power, low-frequency submarine communications transmitter, which was located due north of Shag Slough. The Navy, thinking the official might be on to something, turned off the transmitter for well over an hour, but there was no appreciable response from the whale.

Early on Thursday the rescuers lined up their boats in a neat semicircle upstream of Humphrey, lifted the lengthy pipes over the gunwales, and in unison began banging the pipes with hammers, careful not to make the sound too intense to avoid

Humphrey surfaces in the Sacramento River, ignored by cows grazing in the background.

frightening the animal. Humphrey's response was immediate: He twisted his hulking body and began swimming toward the bridge at the southern end of the slough. The pipes seemed to be working perfectly! But as he approached the bridge, Humphrey refused to go any farther.

"Although the sound of the pipes worked, the whale just balked at the bridge," Stone remembers. "Sometimes it would get quite close, even putting its snout partially through the opening between the bridge pilings, then it would just turn around."

Exasperated officials finally decided to call off the drive temporarily until some of the old pilings could be cleared, perhaps even the bridge itself removed. Many observers felt that Humphrey might have injured himself on the pilings on his original passage into the slough and was afraid to try going the other way.

A crane was brought to the site, and a marine construction crew began clearing a path beneath the bridge. Using underwater sonar to locate sludge and debris, workers labored through the night, removing a substantial amount of sludge,

old pilings and concrete slabs. By dawn, Humphrey had a barrier-free path in the deeper water between bridge poles 11 and 12.

October 25

Pleasant weather continued to hold the next morning, as marine biologists and staff members from the CMMC again positioned their six small boats in a semicircle upstream of Humphrey and began clanging the pipes. California Conservation Corps members waited atop the bridge with a large sheet of weighted plastic to drop over the entrance to the slough should the biologists succeed in moving Humphrey out. Humphrey faced the bridge and, as he had the day before, refused to pass beneath it, much to the dismay of his would-be rescuers. For the next four hours, the pattern was the same. Humphrey swam in lazy circles and figure-eight formations, and the perplexed scientists continued to push.

At one point the lead boat approached too close, and Humphrey let loose a tremendous trumpet blow, a loud, shrill exhalation, which startled the rescuers and may have indicated the giant was getting irritated. Seconds later Humphrey rolled on his side and began slapping the water with his pectoral fins. "Give him 200 yards!" yelled one of the biologists over the walkie-talkie. It was apparent they had pushed too hard, so the operation was halted immediately.

Ken Norris, who had come up from Santa Cruz to check out the situation, said that despite the whale's mud-caked skin and scratched pectoral fins — a result of hitting rocks on the bottom of the shallow slough — Humphrey looked healthy and was acting quite spunky. His skin still showed no ill effects.

At 3 P.M. the drive resumed, this time more intense than ever. The little flotilla pressed closer, one boat almost riding up the animal's back, as the banging of pipes continued. By 3:45 Humphrey once again faced the opening between poles 11 and 12 and, to everyone's relief, tried to pass

The tall blow reveals Humphrey facing the Liberty Island Bridge. For five days, Humphrey was trapped behind this obstacle. Finally, he wriggled through the pilings.

through, only to get momentarily wedged tightly between the poles. With an explosive convulsion that shook the tiny bridge, he wriggled free but did not pass through the opening. Sensing the moment might be near, the rescuers banged the pipes all the louder, pulling the semicircle of boats closer and forcing the giant to attempt a second passage. In what seemed like a desperate attempt to escape the noise of his pursuers, Humphrey blasted through the passage as cheers erupted from the biologists and volunteers. Finally, he was out of the slough. The small boats rushed through the opening in his wake to make sure he didn't decide to turn and head back into the slough that had held him prisoner for almost a week.

For the next three hours Humphrey held a steady course toward Rio Vista, swimming at a brisk four knots; the small escort of boats gathered close behind. Stone and Chorney felt relieved to see the animal heading toward freedom. They were growing increasingly exhausted by the lengthy vigil, which until this moment had been all too frustrating.

As the odd procession moved toward Rio Vis-

ta Bridge in the gloom of early evening, Humphrey disappeared. Despite spotlights and hundreds of eager eyes, even a 45-foot whale can get lost in the dark waters of the Sacramento River. Worried that he might have doubled back to the slough, the flotilla began a sweep of the river with spotlights and flares.

"I was aboard the *Point Heyer* when we received a call from the biologists requesting illumination," Chorney recalls. "We were leading the flotilla about a mile ahead of the small boats and had closed off the Rio Vista Bridge so the traffic wouldn't bother the whale. When we received the request from the small boats, we immediately shot several parachute flares, and the resulting scene looked like something out of the movie *Apocalypse Now*. There were hundreds of people lining the shores and traffic backed up for miles, while on the river there were boats everywhere helped by helicopters with huge spotlights — all searching for a single whale!"

October 26

Morning newspapers across the country reported Humphrey's disappearance. The San Francisco *Examiner* ran a bold headline across the front page: "Where's Humphrey?" But as was to be expected, a 45-foot whale in a narrow river couldn't stay hidden too long. This time it was a foreman on a local farm, Bev Brownell, who first spotted Humphrey, at about 9:20 Saturday morning, swimming back near Liberty Island Bridge. Having read about the oikoime technique in the newspapers, Brownell ran to his small shed and grabbed a pipe of his own. Minutes later he ran down to the water and started "banging like hell" to keep Humphrey from passing back through the pilings that had proved so treacherous the day before. Fortunately, Brownell's makeshift device worked, and Humphrey did not return to the waters of Shag Slough.

A short time later, the biologists once again reformed their line and began driving the whale toward the Rio Vista Bridge several miles to the south. Throughout the day Humphrey repeatedly approached the drawbridge, which was once again raised to stop traffic, but refused to pass beneath it. At one point in mid-afternoon, biologists watched helplessly as the confused giant stranded on a sandbar a short distance north of the bridge, flailing to free himself from the deep river muck. For more than 30 minutes he strained, violently thrashing his tail and blowing frequently, until finally he slid back into deeper water.

Back and forth he swam, a mile or two north, then a sudden turn to the south, shadowed by boats, helicopters, and small planes. But at 4:30 P.M., in an unexpected turn of events, he suddenly swam under the bridge and proceeded south. The second major obstacle had been cleared, and the thousands of onlookers exploded into cheers.

Two large landing craft from the U.S. Army Reserve were quickly dispatched to guide the cetacean into a small bend in the river next to Decker Island called Horseshoe Bend. They hoped to trap him in the bend by closing off both entrances, preventing him from turning upstream under cover of darkness. But even the Army couldn't hold him, and once again Humphrey disappeared.

October 27 through October 29

For the next several days, Humphrey stuck to an exasperating pattern, swimming as much as 15 miles toward the sea, only to return upstream at night, stopping at the bridge at Rio Vista. Much of his time was spent lolling around Decker Island, several miles south of Rio Vista. His behavior kept the biologists guessing.

"The whale may have been using currents for directional orientation, although this is just a theory," Stone points out. "It seemed to be going back and forth against the current, and when the flow slackened, it would get momentarily confused."

Stone's theory is based on studies to determine the ability of baleen whales, and humpbacks in particular, to sense the movement of water through minute hairs on their snouts. These organs may assist them in following migration routes and may explain why Humphrey maintained his perplexing upstream and downstream movements.

Finally, the authorities decided to suspend the operation until a group of whale specialists could meet to think of new solutions. "We drove him as hard as we could," Stone says. "We were as aggressive as we could get. It would have been unfair . . . to continue that stress." Senator Garamendi agreed, noting that even if the whale was not tired, the operation was.

Several days later, after a lengthy conference, the specialists agreed that the whale needed to be moved from the freshwater environment to at least brackish water and, as soon as possible, to salt water. "The unanimous opinion was that the fresh water would ultimately be fatal," Stone notes. "The general feeling was that, for whatever reason, the whale was not able or willing to find its way out and efforts should be continued to move it back to the Pacific."

Based on input from the conference, the Fisheries Service decided to resume the rescue operation in three days using a combination of driving methods. The plan called for the use of at least 20 boats to corral Humphrey, with 10 additional vessels as backup. In addition, the rescuers hoped to dart a tracking device into Humphrey's back to help keep track of him at night and, if necessary, use compressed air explosives to create a sonic barrier to keep him from doubling back upstream.

Meanwhile, Humphrey commercialism continued to thrive. The Point Restaurant sold more Swordfish à la Humphrey than ever, T-shirts continued their brisk sales, and thousands of enthralled spectators clicked their camera shutters every time Humphrey blew or rolled on the surface. One Oakland car dealership ran an ad headlined "Help Us Save Humphrey the Humpback Whale," offering a $100 contribution to the Greenpeace Foundation for every car or truck it sold.

For Chorney and Stone it had been an exhausting ordeal. For the better part of three weeks their days and nights had been consumed by the rescue effort, and despite everything that had been done, the whale was still more than 45 miles from the Pacific. As a result, they were taking everything one day at a time. Their spirits were undoubtedly buoyed, though — both by the dedication of the volunteers and by Humphrey's still vigorous disposition.

November 1

The quiet of this rest day was shattered when the authorities overseeing Humphrey's rescue received a report that a second whale, a 40-foot juvenile gray, had just swum into San Francisco Bay and seemed to be heading in Humphrey's direction. Even though it isn't extremely unusual for grays to come into the bay during their annual migration — the bay probably was a key stopover spot for them before the area was settled — the appearance of the whale at this time seemed more than a coincidence, and officials didn't want to deal with two lost giants at once.

A Coast Guard vessel raced out to intercept the animal and prevent it from heading north into San Pablo Bay, but the officials had nothing to worry about. After spending a few hours spouting and diving around Alcatraz and Angel islands, the gray meandered toward San Francisco's Fisherman's Wharf, delighting hundreds of spectators there before heading seaward beneath the Golden Gate Bridge. Boaters in the bay reported sighting a gray whale throughout the following weekend, but the animal eventually found its way out once and for all.

With one minor crisis averted, attention once again focused on Humphrey. He had moved slightly farther downstream and was spending time frolicking in the San Joaquin River near the small town of Antioch.

November 2

In preparation for the final drive, scientists still hoped to attach a radio transmitter to the whale to enable them to track the animal after dark — an action that seemed at the time to be critical to the success of the overall operation.

Throughout the day, Bruce Mate, who had used the equipment to track humpbacks off Newfoundland, attempted to attach a small crossbow-launched device to the blubber on Humphrey's back, with no success. The device was designed to cling via stainless steel prongs that penetrated the blubber to a depth of about an inch or two, but despite some direct hits, it just wouldn't hold. Sunday's big drive would have to proceed without the services of the transmitter.

November 3

At dawn everything was ready. The armada gathered at Rio Vista looked more ready for a military assault than a whale rescue. The Navy provided 10 river patrol boats, similar to those used on the rivers in Vietnam. These, along with three Army landing craft and two large sportfishing boats, formed a crescent directly behind the whale. Farther back, 20 volunteer vessels formed a second crescent to discourage Humphrey from swimming upstream should he evade the Army/Navy line. Leading the odd caravan downriver, far out in front, was the *Point Heyer*, enforcing the 2,000-yard safety zone that had been declared around the whale that morning.

There had been one major change in plans. Following a suggestion by Lou Herman, a behaviorist from the University of Hawaii known for his advanced and dramatic work on dolphin communication, the authorities decided to try luring Humphrey downstream by using an audio tape of feeding humpbacks instead of driving him with the pipe-banging technique. Herman supplied the recordings, and the Navy provided high-tech underwater speakers and technicians to make sure

the humpback sounds were reproduced as accurately as possible. The Fisheries Service also contracted a noted bioacoustician, Bernard Krause, who has produced sound effects for movies such as *Camelot*, *Rosemary's Baby*, and *Apocalypse Now*, to be in charge of sound reproduction. Krause and the Navy technicians would be directly in front of Humphrey, in the sportfishing boat *Bootlegger*.

After organizing the formation, the *Point Heyer* started moving downriver at about 8 A.M. to clear all boat traffic ahead. By 10 A.M. all was ready to go, so the underwater speakers were turned on and the sounds of feeding humpbacks filtered through the muddy waters of the river.

Humphrey's reaction was almost immediate.

Navy technicians broadcast the sound of feeding whales from the Bootlegger *to lure the errant whale to freedom.*

HUMPHRINA?

About midway through Humphrey's odyssey, as he continued to linger around Decker Island, seemingly uninterested in moving either upstream or downstream, two Office of Emergency Services (OES) employees closely associated with the rescue operation developed a startling theory about the whale. To John and Bev Passerello, Humphrey's penchant for the area seemed territorial, if not downright maternal.

During a several-day halt in the rescue operation, the couple pored over old books about whales and their behavior. A quote from whaler and naturalist Charles M. Scammon particularly caught their eye. In his 1874 book, *The Marine Mammals of the Northwestern Coast of North America*, Scammon wrote: "After many years' study of the characteristic habits of the humpback, we believe that the females of this species resort in large numbers to favorite inland waters, connected with the ocean, to bring forth their young; but there are many exceptions to this rule, incident to their roving disposition."

To the Passerellos, the discovery of this passage shed new light on the saga of Humphrey. Could the whale actually be a pregnant female preparing to give birth in the waters off Decker Island? It seemed a distinct possibility.

Hurriedly, they contacted Stone and told him of their discovery. To him, the thought that Humphrey might be a Humphrina seemed highly unlikely. First of all, humpbacks usually give birth during the months of January, February, and March. Second, Humphrey showed scarring typical of males, and his size seemed to indicate that he was a juvenile, barely beyond the age of puberty. Nevertheless, an estimated 20 percent of female humpbacks are known to bear scars similar to males, so despite his initial skepticism, Stone wanted to review the pregnancy theory, as so little of Humphrey's behavior seemed to make sense anyway. The only way they could sex the animal for sure, however, was to get a good look at its genital region, and no diver was going to attempt that in the muddy wa-

ters of the Sacramento River. All Stone could do was assure the Passerellos he'd investigate their theory further.

Somehow, later that day, the story was leaked to the press, and the Passerellos' quiet theory turned into headlines across the country. Within a day, everyone thought Humphrey was pregnant. The result was a rather uncomfortable situation for both state and federal authorities.

"Suddenly all the press wanted live interviews to confirm the story," Stone recalls. "The Passerellos felt uncomfortable speaking about it to the press because they weren't biologists. Their boss in the OES didn't want to make any statements because he didn't want it to look like the state was saying one thing and the federal government another. It was just blown out of proportion."

With no evidence forthcoming, the media lost interest, and all the furor died down within a day. As was later confirmed, Humphrey turned out to be a he after all.

He shot to the surface and began slapping the water with his pectoral fins. The startled rescuers thought at first that it was an angry response, but moments later Humphrey fell in behind the *Bootlegger*, clearly fascinated by the sounds blasting from the speakers. "He came right up and damn near touched us," blurted one of the boat's biologists over the radio. "He's moving right along; he's eating up our wake."

For the next 12 hours, Humphrey stayed right with the *Bootlegger*, pausing only once or twice, in what seemd like an odd twist of the Pied Piper tale. "We were really surprised at how well the recordings worked," Stone says. "Within a minute or two

the whale responded, then followed the boat for the next 45 miles or so. Occasionally, the sound was turned off so Humphrey wouldn't get too used to it, and he would respond accordingly, slowing or stopping until they turned the sound back on."

Swimming at a brisk four- or five-knot pace, by 8 P.M. Humphrey was enjoying a saltwater environment for the first time in weeks. He swam within four miles of the Golden Gate Bridge before the drive was called off because of darkness. Despite their elation with the drive's progress, the rescuers felt uncertain about what the night would bring. After they lost visual contact with the whale near Angel Island, they worried that once again he would double back and foil the rescue attempt. They had no choice but to wait and see what the morning would bring.

November 4

At 7:30 the following morning Stone was flying high above the bay in a Fish and Game Department plane, trying to locate the whale for what all hoped would be the final run to the Pacific. "I remember hoping that we would find the whale in a reasonable area where we could manage it," Stone says. "It would have been depressing if the animal had returned far upriver again."

As the tiny plane soared over the boat-dotted water, Stone and his pilot found themselves competing for airspace with a slew of media planes and helicopters, crisscrossing paths in a dangerous game to see who could spot the whale first. With so many eyes looking for him, the fickle giant didn't stay hidden long, and by 9 A.M. Stone's plane was circling high over Humphrey, who decided to put on a spectacular show just north of the Richmond–San Rafael Bridge.

"Shortly after we first spotted him," Stone says, "he began breaching repeatedly — a set of eight to ten leaps followed by a short rest period, then another set of breaches. He continued this for about forty-five minutes to an hour, expending tremendous amounts of energy."

Whether Humphrey was annoyed by all the air traffic or just elated to be back in salt water is anyone's guess, but after his tremendous show of energy, it was clear he was quite healthy and suffering few, if any, ill effects from his three weeks in fresh water.

Without hesitation, the flotilla of Navy patrol boats and volunteer vessels converged on the whale, eager to move him the final few miles. But when the *Bootlegger* replayed the feeding humpback sounds, Humphrey showed no interest whatsoever, preferring instead to lounge about the east end of the Richmond–San Rafael Bridge, swimming in circles and blowing contentedly.

"MISS CALIFORNIA ALREADY, DON'T YOU, HUMPHREY.....?"

This cartoon of Humphrey, homesick for sunny California, ran in newspapers across the country.

A quick decision was made to resume the pipe-banging to see if that, combined with the tapes, would start the reluctant cetacean on his way. But Humphrey ignored all efforts on his behalf throughout the morning and into the early afternoon. Finally, at 1 P.M., he swam under the bridge and continued toward the sea at a steady pace.

By 4 P.M. he was nearing the Golden Gate Bridge, where dozens of rush-hour motorists, oblivious to the massive traffic snarl they were causing, stopped their cars and ran to the rails to catch one last glimpse of Humphrey. The official Fisheries Service log notes that he swam beneath the Golden Gate at 4:36 P.M. PST, a full 25 days after his first reported appearance in the bay. Just to make sure he had no surprise U-turns in mind, the escort continued to follow him west. As darkness settled over the fog-shrouded entrance to the bay, Humphrey gracefully lifted his flukes one last time as he disappeared into the depths of the open Pacific. Finally, Fisheries Service agents announced, "It's ended. The boats have broken contact with the whale; they're back, and we've just shut down

As the Bootlegger *leads the way across San Francisco Bay, Humphrey's tail flukes seem to wave good-bye to California.*

the radios — the operation is over."

Stone, who was onshore for the first time in several days as Humphrey made his grand exit, recalled the general feeling of satisfaction. "In the beginning of that day we all knew the drive was working, and as the whale swam the last few miles toward the ocean, my first thought was 'It worked!' Not smugness that we were right all along or anything like that, just a satisfied feeling that the whale was finally in the ocean where it belonged and that all the people who had worked so hard, for whatever reason, could now feel their input was justified."

After 25 days, an estimated $75,000, the involvement of hundreds, perhaps thousands, of volunteers, several politicians, and just about every state and federal agency in California, not to mention the Army, Navy, and Coast Guard, Humphrey, the lost whale, was free.

Stone later tried to put the month into perspective. "The entire rescue operation was unique in the full sense of the word," he said. "I've never had a similar experience that comes close to the rescue of this whale. This was a good news, upbeat thing, as opposed to a disaster, which would normally draw such great crowds. There was nothing to prepare me for the media event it became. The interaction of agencies and people, including both extremes from whale fanatics to skeptics, all pull-

ing together, having a great time, working to save this single whale, was very special."

Stone said Humphrey taught us "bits and pieces" about the behavior and biology of humpbacks. "Basically we learned that a whale can be driven by the dolphin-driving technique and is capable of surviving at least three weeks in fresh water," he said. "In addition, there is some preliminary evidence, although the tapes have not been analyzed, that the whale may have been using some sort of echolocation, or at least frequencies useful for echolocation, something which we are not sure baleen whales are capable of. But the surprising event for all of us was that the use of a positive stimulus, the whale-feeding sounds, was so effective for so long. The successful use of this positive stimulus, as opposed to a negative stimulus, the pipe-banging, will most likely be useful in similar situations in the future."

Humphrey also taught us something about ourselves and how far we've come in a relatively short amount of time. The fact that hundreds of rescuers would come together and spend tremendous time and effort, as well as thousands of dollars, to rescue a single whale says a lot about our concern for the environment. Not a bad legacy for a lost whale! □

WHALE PESTS

No one enjoys the ants that invade in the spring, the mosquitoes that bite all summer, and the mice that nibble in the pantry in the winter. But if you think we've got problems, consider for a moment the creatures that pester whales.

Probably the most visible whale pests are the numerous species of barnacles that burrow into the skin of some of these giants. Generally, the slower swimming whales, such as humpbacks and grays, play host to colonies of barnacles. The average 45-foot humpback, for example, carries about 1,000 pounds of barnacles, including acorn barnacles (three inches across), pseudo-stalked barnacles, and ship barnacles, which grow on the shells of acorn barnacles. These hard-shell crustaceans usually thrive on the whale's head (particularly the chins of humpbacks), flippers, and flukes. They often cover the bodies of gray whales, especially the dorsal area, which is repeatedly exposed to air when the whale surfaces. Barnacles are believed to cause no serious damage, although they do leave noticeable scars when detached.

Right whales, humpbacks, and gray whales also are infested with whale lice, which live off the skin of their hosts. The lice usually are an inch in length and cling to the skin by imbedding their claw-tipped legs; they lurk in the deep skin folds and swarm in profuse numbers on the large callosity on the upper tip of a right whale's snout (which whalemen called the bonnet). As horrible as they sound, lice do not injure the whales. In fact, they

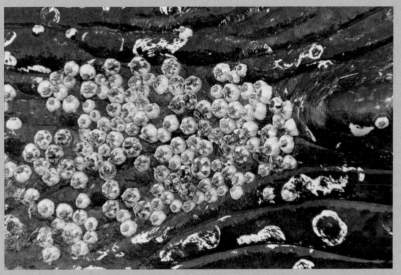

The average humpback carries about 1,000 pounds of barnacles on its body.

actually may help the whale by eating dead skin.

Other pests are more painful. The cookie-cutter shark could be called the whale's version of the mosquito. This two-foot shark, which is found in the warmer parts of the Atlantic and Pacific oceans, attaches its mouth by suction to the skin of whales, and using its razor-sharp teeth, removes a neat oval-shaped scoop of skin and blubber. The resulting wound looks as if someone took a spoon with an extremely sharp edge and scooped out an inch-deep hole. These holes mystified scientists for many years, until in 1971 they were identified as the handiwork of the cookie-cutter shark.

Occasionally, the swords of swordfish are found imbedded in the skin of whales. Most likely these rather uncomfortable encounters happen more by accident than through deliberate attack, since the swordfish also ends up damaged through loss of its sword. Large cetaceans also play host to tapeworms that

could be superstars of the horror movie circuit. One particular species grows to more than 50 feet in length!

Whales have learned to live with barnacles, cookie-cutter sharks, swordfish, and even tapeworms, but they are still getting used to one pest. Although whaling is dying out, that doesn't mean people are coexisting peacefully with whales. Oil-drilling platforms at sea may interfere with migration routes; pollution from nuclear waste and garbage dump sites threatens the fragile ocean environment; overfishing eventually may threaten the whale's food source; and careless boaters and thrill seekers attempting to get a close look at whales may leave scars on their backs or flukes. One humpback off the coast of Maine sports half a fluke, probably from a close encounter with a ship's prop. Sadly, it's people who rank as the whale's greatest pests, not the prolific barnacle hitching a free ride or the cookie-cutter shark with its huge appetite.

RESCUING AN OLD FRIEND

The entire effort seemed at best a long shot. A few people in a tiny Zodiac inflatable boat would try to free a 38-foot humpback whale entangled in a gill net. It seemed impossible, but if they didn't try, it meant sure death for the drowning leviathan. And that would be a bitter loss for the numerous Gulf of Maine scientists on hand.

It was October 23, 1984, and five years to the day since Ibis, the young entangled whale, was first spotted as a calf by members of the Cetacean Research Program at the Provincetown Center for Coastal Studies on Cape Cod. Each summer since then, Ibis had been observed in the rich feeding grounds of the gulf, literally growing up before the eyes of the scientists, who gathered volumes of data on her.

Ibis was named for a black mark on her flukes similar to the hieroglyph of the sacred Egyptian bird. She was the calf of Pegasus, another familiar Gulf of Maine humpback. Ibis was approaching reproductive maturity herself, and cetologists were hoping she would return with a calf the following spring, an event that would give the ongoing research project its first known third-generation whale. But somehow during the summer of 1984, perhaps while feeding deep undersea, Ibis had become entangled in more than 200 feet of gill net, which threatened to tire and drown her.

Ibis was first spotted trailing the net on October 6 by scientists working aboard the research vessel *Dolphin* out of Provincetown. She was later identified from photographs taken at the scene. Two weeks later she was spotted again, still trailing the net, east of Thatcher's Island at the tip of Cape Ann. A couple days later she was sighted from the air in the same vicinity, after a Massachusetts wildlife consortium called I KARE provided an aircraft and pilot for the concerned cetologists at the Provincetown center. Immediately, New England Aquarium divers, in concert with the Coast Guard, attempted to free the actively swimming whale.

They were not successful.

Although her movements were somewhat hampered by the net, Ibis was still capable of swimming freely, and it was difficult to keep a day-to-day fix on her position. Each new day required a new search.

On October 21, a day after the divers failed to free her, she was spotted by naturalists Candice Keays and Howard Garrett from the whale-watching vessel *Privateer* out of Gloucester. She was meandering among numerous lobster buoys, less than 900 feet from Eastern Point in Gloucester.

Immediately, the Provincetown center's director, Charles "Stormy" Mayo, and one of his colleagues, Carole Carlson, left aboard the research vessel *Halos* for the site. When the naturalists in Gloucester lost track of Ibis, the crew of the *Halos* decided to search the eastern edge of Stellwagen Bank, a significant humpback feeding ground along the way. But once again the humpback had given her pursuers the slip.

Nevertheless, plans for her rescue were being formulated. The scientists planned to use an old whaling technique to immobilize Ibis briefly so they could approach her and cut away the net. The Indians and settlers of the New England coast used to catch whales by attaching numerous sealskin or wooden floats with harpoons. As more floats were added, the whale found it increasingly difficult to dive and grew more and more exhausted, until the hunters were able to approach and kill it from their small boats. Similarly, the scientists planned to attach three 50-inch-circumference plastic floats to the net to slow Ibis. Although their motives were dramatically different from those of the hunters of centuries before, one thing hadn't changed: the danger. As friendly and familiar as Ibis was, she was still a 35-ton behemoth who could unwittingly destroy a small boat and its occupants with a flip of her tail.

Mayo contacted Jon Lien, a marine mammal entrapment specialist from Memorial University in Newfoundland, to discuss the situation. Lien

Like Ibis, this humpback in the Gulf of Maine was entangled in a gill net. A line from the net wrapped around its body, pinning its pectoral fin to its side.

strongly recommended against putting any divers in the water near the whale, because they might get tangled in the nearly invisible monofilament net. Any attempt to cut the net would have to take place from a boat at the surface.

Early in the morning on October 23, the crew of the *Halos* spotted Ibis as the boat cleared Gloucester Harbor. She was in worse shape than they had thought. Apparently the trailing net had snagged on the ocean bottom, literally pinning her to the spot and barely allowing her to surface to breathe. A portion of the line went through her mouth and across her back on both sides, like a horse's bridle. When she surfaced to breathe, the line sometimes would pull at her mouth, yanking the struggling animal back underwater headfirst. At other times she would briefly rise horizontally, then pivot to a vertical position as the line seemed to drag her tailfirst to the bottom.

Clearly, she was exhausted. Her blow was weak and V-shaped, evidence she had struggled far too long. A healthy humpback blow usually starts out somewhat wing-shaped and rises to a vertical bushy plume as the blow pressure increases. It was all too clear that Ibis might soon drown.

There wasn't a moment to waste. After preparing all the necessary gear, three rescuers climbed into the Zodiac *Olympia* for the first attempt. Perran Ross, a specialist from Gloucester's Ocean Research and Education Society, would attempt to attach the floats with an eight-foot pole from his position in the bow; Carlson sat in the middle of the boat to ensure that all lines stayed clear; and Mike Williamson of the Massachusetts-based Mingan Island Cetacean Study, who was recruited for the task because of his expertise in operating Zodiacs near blue, fin, and humpback whales, was at the controls.

The tiny craft approached the entangled whale slowly to avoid panicking her further. "OK, Mike, she's off your port side now," yelled Ross, as he guided Williamson in toward the animal. "Careful now. Slowly. She's right in front of us!"

Deftly, Williamson tried to maneuver the inflatable to a position right over the whale, who remained submerged to avoid the vessel. They made repeated passes, but each time she stayed just out of reach. At one point, Carlson held Ross's kicking legs as he dangled over the side in a desperate attempt to grab the submerged line. Finally, Ross was able to attach the floats, only to have them break free minutes later.

For hours the rescue attempts continued, and each time the crew grew bolder in its approach as it raced against the clock. For a tense moment, observers on the *Halos* held their breath as Ibis surfaced tailfirst and slowly lifted her flukes directly over the boat; a ton or so of whale was poised to crush the comparatively tiny occupants. Seconds

Stormy Mayo (right) *and David Mattila, with the* Halos *in the background.*

later she eased beneath the surface, curling her flukes to avoid hitting the boat.

Then the boat's engine stalled. As Williamson struggled with the motor, the exasperated crew watched as Ibis bobbed to the surface for a long breath. Finally an excellent opportunity to attach the floats, and they couldn't get near her.

Mayo decided to call the *Olympia* back to the *Halos* to devise a second, more ambitious plan. Since everyone felt it was only a matter of minutes before she drowned, Mayo planned to drive the inflatable practically up on the back of the animal in an aggressive attempt to attach the floats. This time he would take the bow position. Minutes later the two rescuers motored off toward the whale, but while the rescuers were consulting, Ibis had disappeared. Had the net pulled away from the bottom, allowing her to swim away, or had it dragged her to the bottom for the final time?

For the next day and a half the puzzled scientists conducted an intensive search of the area, aided by several experienced spotters aboard commercial whale-watching vessels. Despite excellent sea conditions, Ibis could not be found, so it was presumed she had drowned and sunk. On October 25, the disheartened crew of the *Halos* returned to Provincetown.

In his official report of the rescue attempt, Mayo added a personal note: "To the population of humpback whales in the North Atlantic, the death of Ibis would be a loss; to those of us who have studied Ibis since she was a young calf, her loss would be a profound tragedy."

A month later, on Thanksgiving Day, the *Halos* departed from its home dock for a routine late season cruise. Just outside the harbor, the crew spotted several humpbacks. As he has thousands of times in the past, Mayo focused his telephoto lens on the animals to secure some ID photographs for the center's files. What he saw this time sent a tremendous rush of adrenalin through his system. One of the animals was Ibis! For a brief moment before she dove, he recognized the net and cork line that still trailed behind her. "I was shocked," he says. "We were almost sure she had drowned!"

Immediately, the crew swung into action. While the *Halos* remained at the scene, volunteers rushed back to port in the *Olympia* to pick up the necessary rescue gear and additional help. Within an hour, the *Olympia* returned, accompanied by a second Zodiac named, appropriately, *Ibis,* in honor of what the cetologists had thought was their drowned friend. This time Ibis was not anchored to one spot, and Mayo and his crew would have to attach the floats to a free-swimming whale. It was a tremendously dangerous challenge but one, thought Mayo, well worth the risk.

By now the trailing net had snagged dozens of dogfish sharks, which made the whale's swimming labored and difficult. If something weren't done right away, Mayo suspected, Ibis probably would die on the upcoming 2,000-mile migration south to the Caribbean.

Ibis was swimming with a second whale, a large male known to the cetologists as Blizzard. Mayo and his colleagues were unsure how Blizzard would react when they approached Ibis, so they had to be very cautious when the chase began.

Since Ibis was swimming free, the initial plan called for the Zodiacs to chase her until she showed some signs of exhaustion. Then, David Mattila, director of Caribbean research for the center, would try to attach the floats and clip the net free.

Fortunately, the weather and sea conditions favored the chase. The Zodiacs flew over the

Rescuers from the Center for Coastal Studies approach Ibis. A normal humpback blow shoots straight up, like a geyser. Ibis's low, bushy blow indicates that she had grown very weak.

smooth Atlantic water as the fall air whipped the faces of the rescuers. Ibis and her companion were trying their best to evade the pursuers, but the surfacing habits of humpbacks are predictable to experienced observers such as Mayo and Mattila. It wasn't long before she had tired. Blizzard seemed to have decided to watch the proceedings, making no effort to disturb them.

In a way, Mayo's rescue attempt was in the tradition of his Cape Cod ancestors, Provincetown fishermen who would go whaling when the opportunity presented itself, using techniques much like these. Mayo even has a photograph of his father posing with four pilot whales he'd captured decades ago. Now, Mayo points out, his father is one of the center's most enthusiastic supporters.

Despite her growing exhaustion, Ibis was proving extremely difficult to catch, so Mayo and Mattila decided to try to catch the trailing net with a pronged anchor, then haul the boat toward her. After two throws, the anchor caught. An attached pink buoy marking Ibis's location went flying over

the waves, and Mayo tied off the other end of the 200-foot line. A modern Nantucket sleigh ride began, as the whale towed the small boat, rising and diving. After several minutes, the crew of the *Olympia* was able to haul in close enough to attach three large buoys to the trailing net. Ibis dove once again, but the tremendous drag of the buoys discouraged her, and after another 30 minutes, she lay still in the water. The time had come to cut the net.

Mayo maneuvered the *Olympia* close enough to feel the salty spray of the leviathan's labored blow. Mattila crouched in the bow, knife in hand, waiting for an opportunity to cut the net. Between blows, Ibis dropped a few feet below the surface, enabling Mayo practically to row the inflatable over her submerged back.

On the first approach, Ibis surfaced within inches of the bow, so Mattila quickly reached over and cut the first section of line with his long steel knife. As his shout of success echoed over the water, cheers erupted on the *Halos*.

Mayo felt that to remove the net completely,

he would first have to take it out of Ibis's mouth and then pull it back toward the tail. To do this, Mattila hopped into the *Ibis* to begin cutting the line up toward the whale's head, while Mayo remained back toward the tail in the *Olympia*, preventing as best he could any further entanglement of the tail. According to Mayo, the view of the whale from that angle was "staggering." The enormity of both their subject and the project at hand seemed overwhelming, but as tired as she was, Ibis was cooperating.

While Mayo kept a close watch on the flukes, which at times draped over their bow, Mattila and the *Ibis* crew approached the whale's enormous head. Shouting directions to the helm, Mattila lunged to grab the line that wound through the animal's jaws; he pulled it up as the whale ponderously surfaced. With a flash of his knife, he severed the line, and cheers again erupted from the *Halos.*

Mattila braced himself to pull the line through the cetacean's mouth, but Ibis kept her jaws clamped tight, unaware of how close she was to ridding herself of the net. Mattila pleaded with her to open her mouth as he yanked. He knew the line was wedged deep into her baleen and would never float free — he had to get it out. It wouldn't be long before Ibis recovered her strength and attempted to swim off, so it had to be done now.

Desperately, Mattila heaved on the line, gathering in as much as he could when Ibis surfaced. When she submerged again, he braced the line against the side of the inflatable until it threatened to pull the boat under. Mattila's arms ached as the line creaked and groaned against the gunwale. Then, a few feet below the surface, Ibis unexpectedly opened her mouth. Mattila stumbled back and then recovered enough to pull the line completely through.

"It's free!" he shouted. The jubilant rescue crew easily removed the remainder of the net, and Ibis was free. At first she moved tentatively, still gathering her strength; then she rejoined Blizzard and disappeared over the horizon.

During the weeks that followed, Ibis was sighted several times just north of Cape Cod on Stellwagen Bank. Her rescuers at the center worried that the months of entrapment in the net might have prevented her from gaining the weight necessary for the long southward migration. Still, she was free and capable of feeding; perhaps she would recoup the weight she had lost.

Winter arrived, and Ibis disappeared with the other Gulf of Maine humpbacks. The staff at the center, along with other New England cetologists, eagerly awaited spring and a chance to look for Ibis. Then they would know for sure whether the rescue had succeeded.

The next spring, on a commercial whale watch out of Gloucester, Candice Keays and Mike Williamson, who were both involved in the initial rescue attempt, were watching several humpbacks frolic in the icy gulf waters. Then a familiar fluke appeared. It was Ibis. "Seeing her was the biggest emotional rush of my life," Williamson recalls. "That first true confirmation that she had lived through the winter meant a lot to all of us. She is a very special humpback."

News of her arrival caused a celebration at the Provincetown center. The crew had saved a whale that was not only scientifically significant but also an old friend. At the same time, they had developed a proven method for freeing entangled whales, one that they would use over the next year to free two other well-known humpbacks.

Aboard the whale watch, Keays pulled out a bottle of champagne and toasted their success. On the bottle was a special label attached weeks earlier. It read, "Open in case of Ibis." □

SAVED BY A BAND-AID

When stories of dramatic marine mammal rescues hit the newspapers, they usually originate from coastal locations. But one such heartwarming tale took place in Apple Valley, Minnesota, more than 1,000 miles from the nearest ocean. At the Minnesota Zoological Garden, a 14-foot, 1,800-pound male beluga whale nicknamed Big Mouth was saved through the combined efforts of the zoo's veterinarian and volunteers, a concerned surgeon, and a corporate giant whose medical specialists designed a whale-size Band-Aid.

In 1984, a small cut appeared on Big Mouth's lower lip. Zoo officials suspected he had banged his lip on the metal feeding platform of his tank. At first there was no cause for alarm. Both Big Mouth and his companion, Little Girl, had had minor cuts before, and they had healed quickly. But over the next several months, the small cut grew to a festering two-inch sore, which threatened the animal's life.

A year after the cut first appeared, the 15-year-old mammal (whose official name is *Nukilik*, meaning "strong" in Eskimo) was given only a 50-50 chance for survival. An analysis of his blood showed a dangerously low count of red and white blood cells, and he was suffering from respiratory inflammation and gastritis.

Enter Dr. David Knighton, a surgeon from the University of Minnesota. Spurred by his patients, who were calling him to ask whether he could do something to save the whale, Dr. Knighton contacted zoo officials and offered to help. He mixed a

The beluga nicknamed Big Mouth, with the special bandage attached to his lip.

sample of the whale's blood with a variety of chemicals to make a salve designed to stimulate the natural healing process, a treatment he often had used on human patients with similar slow-healing wounds.

In order for the salve to work, though, a bandage was required to hold it in place. But where do you find a whale-size Band-Aid? Zoo officials found the answer in their own backyard. The 3M Company in nearby St. Paul, best known for Scotch tape, put its Medical-Surgical Division to work solving the problem.

The 3M Company specialists developed an experimental four-by-eight-inch moisture-resistant bandage designed to protect the whale's wound from the chemicals in its tank. The bandage would have to stick to Big Mouth's slippery skin, despite the fact that whale skin sloughs off extremely rapidly.

To apply the salve and ban-

dage, zookeepers drained Big Mouth's 30,000-gallon holding tank, propped up his flukes and head on foam cushions (to protect him from his own weight), towel-dried the wound, and began treatment. The whale's companion, Little Girl, was kept nearby to reduce Big Mouth's stress.

The bandages would stay on about half a day before the beluga, irritated by the loosening bandage flaps, would shake his head vigorously and scrape them off. They were replaced twice a day, as volunteers lay next to the "beached" whale, uttering soothing assurances. Protected by the bandage, Big Mouth's wound soon showed signs of new tissue growth. After several weeks, Big Mouth was well enough to return to his tank, and one year later, surgeons removed the damaged tissue in an unprecedented operation. Now Big Mouth is back on display.

On the trail of whales, I've had the opportunity to travel to many places, meet all sorts of fascinating people, and see some remarkable sights. But for sheer primitive natural beauty, few places have touched me as deeply as Lubec, Maine.

Here the earth meets the sea as only God could have planned it. Tall cliffs, laden with evergreens dwarfed and bent by the fierce northeast storms, conceal deep fjordlike coves where bald eagles soar and surf thunders ashore. Here there are whirlpools and fierce currents caused by the greatest tide changes in the country.

This coast, the easternmost point in the United States, remains an untouched wilderness, overlooking the tide-ripped waters of the Bay of Fundy, a shallow, nutrient-rich body of water that's home to hundreds, perhaps thousands, of whales, as great a concentration of these mammals as anywhere on earth. Humpbacks, finbacks, minkes, right whales, white-sided dolphins, and harbor porpoises abound in these waters through the summer and fall, swimming and feeding within sight of the rockbound coast.

Here, too, fishermen harvest great quantities of the herring that attract many of these whales to Lubec, and herein lies a conflict. For when man and whale both live off the sea's offerings in a small area, conflict is almost inevitable.

The problems begin when the whales move inshore to pursue herring. An adult humpback can consume more than 2,000 pounds of fish per day, and in its blind pursuit of food, it sometimes blunders into the fishing gear set by the locals. Even if it doesn't destroy the gear completely, it often becomes hopelessly entangled, creating a problem for the owner: What do you do with a trapped 40-ton giant?

That's where Edwin "Butch" Huntley comes in. In similar situations elsewhere in the world fishermen might shoot the whale in an attempt to save their gear. In Lubec, the fishermen rely on

Lubec, Maine.

Huntley to resolve whale entrapments amicably.

Using techniques developed by biologists such as Jon Lien, who has spent years teaching Newfoundland fishermen how to free trapped whales, Huntley has freed more than 25 whales, making him a local hero of sorts. In fact, a large mural, painted on a dilapidated storefront on Lubec's Water Street, depicts Huntley at the helm of his boat, *Seafarer*, pursuing a whale. One incident in particular offers a vivid example of his work. Huntley was called to free a humpback trapped in a weir, a 50-foot-wide herring trap formed by wooden poles driven into the sea floor.

Huntley recalls, "They had already tried to purse the animal out the opening, which means slowly closing a net toward the entrance to the weir. But it only spooked the whale, and he tore the six-thousand-dollar purse to shreds." Huntley and Greg Stone, a New England Aquarium researcher, decided to remove a few of the weir's poles and some of the twine, and somehow lure the whale out the opening.

Huntley continues: "While we were getting our diving gear on, one of the other researchers on the scene hands me this pen-shaped object and asks if I would get a skin sample from the whale. 'All you do,' she said, 'is poke the animal with the sharp end, twist, and pull, and it will take a three-eighth-inch core sample.' "

"Now stabbing a forty-five-foot whale in a fifty-foot enclosure was not my idea of fun," Huntley says, "and I told her that despite their size, they have extremely sensitive skin. In fact, it makes you feel awfully insignificant when you touch one of those giants anywhere and their skin shimmers to the touch. They're very sensitive. But in the interest of science, I told her I'd give it a try."

The visibility underwater was about 20 feet, but the humpback almost filled the weir. A couple of times it brushed Huntley with its barnacled flippers, ripping holes in his dry suit and bruising him. Nonetheless, the two men were able to clear an opening in the weir. They decided to lie at the bottom of the opening and use their scuba regulators to create a mass of bubbles to attract the whale to the escape route.

"So here I am," Huntley says, "lying on the bottom, when suddenly I look up and there's this massive snout staring down at me less than two feet away. You can imagine the feeling that came over me seeing this 40-ton giant hovering just inches away — and here I am with this ridiculous core sampler in my hand. I looked at that massive snout looking down at me, looked at the sampler, and thought, 'You're a fool if you do because he'll drive you and your silly sampler two feet into the mud.' Needless to say, they didn't get their skin sample."

When the tide came in a little farther, the humpback swam out the opening, and after hanging around the weir for a short time, it took off for the open sea.

A commercial diver and fisherman, Huntley is a colorful character whose powerfully built five-foot nine-inch frame, callused hands, and weathered face bespeak years of seagoing experience. His expertise and unflappable self-confidence have earned him the respect of his peers in an environment in which respect, like the living, doesn't come easy.

Lubec's hard times are clearly evident in the abandoned sardine canneries that sit like bleached skeletons on the waterfront. The Peacock Canning Company on Water Street and Booth Fisheries on

Edwin "Butch" Huntley at the helm of his fishing boat, the Seafarer.

Commercial Street are all that remain of a once-thriving sardine packing industry, which not too long ago kept 20 plants in Lubec busy. As it has for decades, the town lives and dies with the sardine industry, and whether there's going to be food on the table depends largely on how the herring are running.

In this difficult situation, it's easy to understand why whales and seals are not always welcome visitors. To the locals they represent direct competition, and to this day nearby Canadian fishermen continue to shoot seals in an effort to increase their catches.

The late summer and fall is spawning time for herring along the coastal areas of Maine and Canada's maritime provinces, and to harvest the vast schools of fish, many fishermen build weirs, a technique first used by the Indians of the Northeast long before Europeans settled the New World. Although weirs vary somewhat from place to place, they commonly consist of a fence of 40- to 50-foot wooden poles driven into the sea floor in roughly the shape of a heart about 50 feet in diameter. Leading into the indent of the heart are sever-

A minke whale chased herring into this weir in Lubec and became trapped. Huntley freed the whale before it could damage the expensive weir.

al leader poles, which point toward shore. Brush or netting is strung between these poles to form a wall. The weirs are set up in coves frequented by herring, and when the small fish run into the leader poles and netting, they swim into the center of the pound, where the walled enclosure traps them. After several days, the herring are retrieved from the weir by carrier boats. Each weir represents an investment of between $25,000 and $50,000 for the owner, but with a good season's catch of herring, the return on investment is substantial.

What may wreck this simple, effective fishing technique is, of course, a hungry whale. Once trapped inside a weir, the whale too becomes confused and unable to escape. Although not actually entangled in the net, the whale will swim about within the enclosure, devouring the herring and attempting escape until finally, either frustrated or hungry, it simply swims through the weir, destroying everything.

When Huntley first moved into the area, he had no idea he would someday be freeing whales. Although he was born and raised in Boston, Huntley's family had been fishermen and boatbuilders in Lubec for many generations, and throughout his youth, Huntley spent his summers here learning the skills of his forebears. When he decided to

return to his ancestral home in 1970, no one was surprised. Now he makes his living like almost everybody else in Lubec — he fishes — but his diving experience brings in additional income from repairing, retrieving, or installing fishing gear. No one pays him for freeing whales, though. Huntley is motivated only by his concern for the giants, an interest that began in the late 1970s, when Lubec's whales became the center of controversy over an oil refinery proposed for nearby Eastport.

In 1980, because of the possible negative effects of the refinery and the increased shipping traffic on the right whale population there, the National Marine Fisheries Service contracted with Boston's New England Aquarium to determine the number of cetacean species present in the lower Bay of Fundy. During the aerial and shipboard surveys over the next few years, researchers first observed large numbers of right whales summering there, an exciting find that New England Aquarium director Dr. John Prescott characterizes as "probably the most important cetacean discovery in the past twenty or twenty-five years." Right whales once existed in large numbers throughout New England waters, but overzealous whaling reduced the population so much that for a 100-year period ending in 1955, none were reported off New England, despite full protection from whaling since 1937.

Subsequent observations of the animals mating, nursing, and rearing calves in the waters of the Bay of Fundy provided the final evidence that the Eastport-Lubec area was a critical habitat for the whales, which was enough to shelve the idea of the oil refinery. Since then several researchers have continued to monitor the bay's right whale population, identifying more than 200 individuals.

From the beginning Huntley worked with the researchers and as a result became something of a naturalist himself, learning the various species and their habits. Through his contacts with the fishermen, he also helped the scientists find the varying locations of the whales throughout the season.

"When I freed my first whale about fifteen years ago," Huntley says, "like any other diving work I do, I was paid for it and wasn't even remotely aware of the type of whale that was trapped. In essence, I was being paid to save the fishing gear, not the whale. After assisting the re-searchers, though, I began to see the animals in a different light. Now, when I'm called by a weir owner who has accidentally caught himself a whale, I want to save the whale as much as the fishing gear — and I don't get paid."

Huntley says the fishermen of Lubec don't always consider the whales a nuisance and in fact sometimes see them as just the opposite. "Actually, herring fishermen like to see whales because it means there's fish in the area, despite the fact that they mean competition. I mean, you're not happy when a whale destroys your fifty-thousand-dollar weir, but that's the exception rather than the rule. Usually, the whales drive the herring right into the weir simply by their presence.

"I remember one time a few years back when I was setting up a weir near White Rock with my friend Denny Matthews. I had just finished tying off the bottom of the net and was swimming back to the boat when I saw all these herring swimming under me.

"I hollered over to Denny to turn on his fish finder [an electronic instrument that locates

Huntley's boat, the Seafarer (above), *steams through Lubec Narrows to go to sea.*

A mural of Huntley and the Seafarer (right), *painted on a downtown storefront.*

Researchers aboard the Nereid, *a New England Aquarium vessel.*

schooling fish], and he yells back, 'There's solid herring all the way to the bottom!' That was in twenty-five feet of water. We filled the weir and got another net and sealed off the cove. It was a fishing bonanza — and that was in mid-afternoon. Herring usually don't enter the coves until nightfall. Then we saw the reason why. Just outside the cove were two whales who were obviously scaring the fish right into our nets."

"When the whales do get caught, though, the owner has a real problem," Huntley says. "It's not easy, say, if you have a forty-five-foot humpback penned inside a fifty-foot weir — there's not much room for the animal to move. They'll usually remain satisfied until the food runs out. Then they just bulldoze right through the weir, tearing it all to hell. Sometimes they'll get tangled up and drown."

Freeing these giants obviously is dangerous, even under the best conditions, but the waters of the Bay of Fundy offer additional peril: life-sapping cold as low as 42 degrees Fahrenheit, limited visibility, and tempestuous tides. Huntley has had to learn to cope with these conditions and even to use them to his advantage. It's not unusual, for example, for Huntley to cut the weir netting just low enough to let a trapped whale swim to freedom at the highest tide.

His familiarity with the different species of whales helps him judge their behavioral patterns before devising a plan to free them. Humpbacks, for example, seem to him to be much more intelligent than other species and therefore easier to work with; they seem to act docile because they're aware that the diver is trying to help them. Right whales are, according to Huntley, "the cows of the sea": slow swimming and somewhat stupid. Minkes, the fast, 30-foot baleen whales, seem hyperactive and skittish.

For all the obvious dangers involved in freeing a trapped whale, Huntley's most frightening encounter occurred in the open waters off Lubec while he was accommodating a photographer taking some underwater pictures of a right whale for the *Providence* (R.I.) *Sunday Journal.* The resulting incident gave them both quite a scare and remains to this day one of Huntley's favorite stories.

In the fall of 1981, Huntley joined photographer Jim Daniels and six researchers aboard the New England Aquarium's 28-foot fiberglass boat *Nereid* in search of right whales. The aquarium crew had reluctantly agreed to let Daniels try to photograph the animals underwater if the opportunity presented itself. Because of his experience diving with whales, Huntley was asked along.

The boat cruised the waters off a set of small uninhabited islands called The Wolves, just over nine miles off the coasts of Maine and New Brunswick, until in the early afternoon, one of the crew spotted a blow off the stern. As the boat inched closer, the scientists recognized the right whale calf they had nicknamed Snotnose a few weeks before. It was slightly larger than the boat, and as it began rolling alongside and circling the vessel, it obviously was in a playful mood. The mother was nowhere to be seen.

Recognizing a golden opportunity, Huntley and Daniels quickly donned their gear and slipped into the frigid 50-degree water. Because bubbles from scuba regulators seem to frighten whales, they chose to snorkel at the surface, hoping to approach the animal close enough for a decent

A right whale surfaces in the Bay of Fundy. Note the twin blow holes and the giant callosities on its brow, both characteristic of these whales.

photograph. Visibility in the plankton-rich water was limited to less than 15 feet, so they would have to get very close. The calf, meanwhile, was cooperating nicely; at one point it approached the *Nereid* near enough to have its rubbery black back stroked by one of the crew.

Both snorkelers swam over to where they had last seen the calf dive and waited, bobbing at the surface and gazing down into the sunlight-streaked depths. Daniels recalls how quiet everything seemed at that point; he could feel his heart pounding nervously. He wondered what the whale was thinking as it hid in the murkiness below. As was his habit when diving with whales in limited visibility, Huntley slowly rotated in the water, trying to avoid any unwanted surprises.

Out of the green haze below, the calf suddenly appeared, its massive body cruising by the snorkelers almost within touching distance. Characteristically, the calf was showing more curiosity than fear as its 30-ton body glided by. The divers barely had time to exchange excited looks before the animal reappeared within inches of their face masks. As it passed, Huntley imagined himself at a railroad crossing watching a train go by. When the flukes were almost upon Daniels, the calf gently rolled so that the tail turned vertically, in what

seemed like an obvious attempt to avoid hitting the comparatively tiny snorkeler. Again it was gone, leaving the divers gently wallowing in its wake.

"Over the years I've been in a lot of situations where whales could have easily killed me," Huntley says. "A flick of the tail, a nudge from a fin, and they can break you in two. Yet always at the critical moment, they seem to avoid hitting you." Nonetheless, when the divers popped to the surface, Huntley cautioned Daniels about getting too close to the whale's flukes and fins. A hit, however accidental, could be disastrous.

On the third approach, the calf appeared again beneath the snorkelers, but this time, instead of gliding by, it hovered below them, rising slowly like a surfacing submarine, enabling both men almost to stand on its back. Gently they slid into the water beneath the flukes as the animal edged forward. This remarkable activity continued for the next several minutes. At one point while circling, it even flexed its head back as if to chase its tail, with Huntley and Daniels in the center of the circle.

By now much of their fear had disappeared and both men were feeling more comfortable in the bitterly cold, alien environment. Still, with a caution honed by experience, Huntley continued

Despite their rotund shape and huge bulk, right whales are among the most acrobatic of whales.

his 360-degree vigil, just to be sure. The mother had not yet appeared.

"By then we were about one hundred yards from the boat," Huntley recalls. "The calf had pulled its usual disappearing act, and I was staring down past my flippers waiting for it to reappear below us. Instead, this unbelievably massive head, more than twice the size of the calf's, came bolting up from below, just in front of me. Instinctively, I reached out to push away from it as hard as I could, and when I did, I crashed into Daniels, who was just behind me.

"The mother, I guess, finally decided to see what we were all about. It seemed like we were lost in bubbles and foam as she shot about twenty feet out of the water just a few feet from us. She scared the hell out of me — all I could think of was to get back to the boat!

"We swam hard for the *Nereid,* and as I grabbed the ladder, here comes Jim right up over my shoulders and into the boat. He left flipper prints right up my back!"

Moments later, the two whales swam off quietly, leaving two bug-eyed adventurers with racing hearts and a new story to tell. "After I sat down and thought about it," Huntley says. "I realized it was just a motherly thing to do. But when the mother is sixty feet long and weighs sixty tons, that sort of display can take a few years off your life!"

Despite the occasional unnerving encounter, Huntley remains fond of the whales, and he points out that many of the Lubec fishermen, who in previous years held a less than enthusiastic view of the giants, are now showing an increased interest. "When I used to get calls from other fishermen to tell me they'd spotted whales," Huntley says, "I'd ask them what kind, and they'd say, 'Oh geez, I don't know, they're whales!' Now a lot of them are starting to recognize the different species, and their cooperation in locating the animals has really helped the research efforts a lot." □

THE ICEBERG WHALE

Despite all his experience freeing whales, Butch Huntley would have been at a loss if he'd been called in April 1985 when fishermen off the tiny Greenland settlement of Alluitsup discovered the body of a 60-foot male sperm whale stranded on an iceberg. Whale strandings in the area are common, but this one was highly unusual: The animal lay frozen in ice more than 13 feet above the water.

The story ran in newspapers all over the United States with the headline "Whale Found in Iceberg Puzzles Experts." Marine biologists called to the scene wondered how old the animal was, how it died, and, most intriguing, how it ended up 13 feet above the water's surface.

At first some theorized that the whale was a prehistoric specimen buried for thousands of years somewhere in the Greenland ice cap, which covers 85 percent of the island. They figured the ice in which the whale lay entombed split off and floated away as an iceberg. Biologists on the scene quickly dismissed that idea, however, because the animal in no way differed from contemporary sperm whales, and in any case, its overpowering stench indicated it was no fossil.

What they did find was a large cylindrical hole 15 inches in diameter and three feet deep in the side of the whale's head, which seemed to local photographer John Rasmussen, one of the first people on the scene, like the wound left by a grenade-tipped harpoon. That would explain the whale's death. But how did it get so high above the waterline?

One theory suggested the

Scientists examine the carcass of a sperm whale trapped on an iceberg near Greenland.

whale breached next to the iceberg, landing high on the ice and getting wedged into a small crevasse. Although this may sound possible, it would be quite a feat for a 60-foot whale to breach with enough power to land high and dry 13 feet above the water. What's more, this whale lay with its tail toward the center of the iceberg, which meant the animal would have had to breach 13 feet in the air tailfirst — an impossible feat.

While experts pondered the origin of the animal, local residents worked with saws and crowbars to remove the whale's ivory teeth, which they would make into the carvings they call *tupilaks*. Since sperm whales were protected from whaling by international law the teeth have become a prize rarity, for which the natives receive $25 apiece, which helps them purchase food, fuel, and ammunition for their hunting rifles.

After a lengthy examination of both the whale and the surrounding ice, marine biologists Lars Haumann and Finn Kapel from Greenland's Fisheries and Environmental Research Institute, solved the bizarre mystery of the iceberg whale.

They believe the dead or dying animal, which may have been illegally harpooned, was drifting near the iceberg when the ice suddenly calved, or split, and rolled over. The whale then was lifted up on the previously submerged portion of the ice. Then the iceberg and its "involuntary hitchhiker," as one reporter described the whale, drifted south with the polar current between Greenland and Iceland, finally stranding just past Cape Farvel on the southern tip of the island, where it was discovered by fishermen in early April. Old waterline marks on the ice just above the whale's resting place provided the answer to the perplexing mystery.

In mid-April, a powerful storm out of the southeast freed the iceberg, carrying it and its unusual passenger far beyond the curious gaze of man, thus ending one of the world's most unusual stranding cases.

THE RIGHT WHALE

Eubalaena glacialis
("True whale in icy water")

Approximate maximum length & weight: 58 feet, 100 tons.

Coloring: Black with white patches underneath.

Food: Microscopic creatures such as copepods and euphausids.

Distribution: Along major land masses in temperate oceans of both hemispheres.

Estimated maximum age: None available, although a member of the right whale family, the bowhead, is believed to live as long as 40 years.

Description: Right whales are perhaps the most unusual looking whales. They are extremely fat and rounded with large, light-colored growths, called callosities, on their heads. The location of these hardened patches corresponds roughly to the location of facial hair on humans: above the eyes, on the chin and jaw, and forward of the nostrils. These callosities are infested with whale lice and sometimes barnacles, and they vary enough in shape and location to allow scientists to identify individual whales. Other distinctive features include the paddle-shaped flippers, a highly arched mouth, and lack of a dorsal fin. When feeding, right whales skim the surface with their enormous mouths open, fil-tering out bushels of microscopic plankton with finely fringed black baleen.

Right whales are extremely slow swimmers, seldom exceeding 4 miles per hour, although they are capable of short bursts up to 12 miles per hour. When diving, they arch their backs prominently, finally lifting their broad, triangular tail flukes high in the air. Because their nostrils are farther apart than most baleen whales', their blow is distinctively V-shaped.

Despite their rotund size, right whales are fairly acrobatic, prone to breaching, flipper slapping, and lobtailing. Zoologist Roger

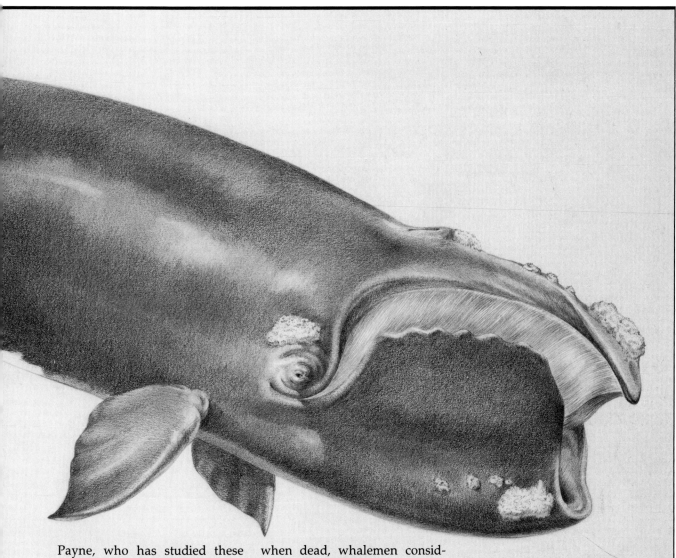

Payne, who has studied these creatures extensively, says they also like to engage in a form of "wind sailing" with their wide flukes, which involves "standing" on their heads and letting the wind catch their flukes and push them along. They often will swim back to the starting point to begin the maneuver again.

Calves are born in warm waters during the winter after a gestation of just under 12 months. Newborns are generally 16 to 19 feet long and will remain with their mothers throughout the first year.

Because they yielded the highest amount of oil and floated when dead, whalemen considered them the "right" whale to kill. Their slow swimming habits made them easy prey, and as a result, the worldwide population was decimated. Despite protection since 1937, their slow reproductive rate and possible competition for food from sei whales make right whales the world's most endangered great whales, with fewer than 2,000 animals left.

OPERATION BELUGA

The ice-encrusted shores and frozen tundra of the Arctic basin make it an unforgiving place. Scant sunlight and severe cold make life difficult for man and beast alike. So it was with great joy that Vasili Peliachaivyn, a native hunter of the Chukchi Peninsula in the eastern Soviet Union, returned from a successful hunt along the coast during the exceptionally cold December of 1984.

Peliachaivyn is one of the "People of the Long Spring," an arctic tribe closely tied to the sea and its animals, who believe that spring, which comes with the first sun after the long polar night, is their longest season. Their legends say the coastal Chukchi people originated with the mating of the spirit mother and a whale, who changed into a man for the purpose.

Like all his people, Peliachaivyn was intimately familiar with the sea and its many moods and creatures, but he was unprepared for the sight that would greet him shortly.

The lone hunter's dogsled raced across the ice of the barren wilderness, both master and his dogs looking forward to the warmth of home. Abruptly, the powerful dogs stopped, and the sled ground to an unexpected halt. The animals stood motionless, staring out over the dark waters of Senyavina Strait, a narrow strip of icy water directly across the Bering Strait from Alaska.

Peliachaivyn was puzzled by the behavior of his dogs, but then he heard a strange sound rising above the whistle of the chill arctic wind. A drawn-out moan emanated from the direction of the strait; the eerie, almost humanlike groan reminded Peliachaivyn of the sound of walruses, but they had departed the area for the season. Intrigued, he pulled out his binoculars and searched the blue water and its shifting fields of ice for the origin of the moaning. What he saw filled him at first with joy, then with alarm.

Swimming a short distance from shore was a herd of white beluga whales, or "polar dolphins" as the Chukchi call them. At first Peliachaivyn thought the whales were playing, but further inspection convinced him they were in serious trouble. Exceptionally strong easterly winds had shifted the massive ice fields, trapping scores of belugas in shrinking pools of open water, gradually cutting off their air supply.

The gathering of belugas at these *savssats*, or ice holes, in unusually cold weather is not rare, because the mammals lack the lung capacity of their larger cousins. But Peliachaivyn was stunned by the enormous number of whales he saw. There were hundreds, perhaps thousands!

Under normal circumstances, this might have been a bonanza for Peliachaivyn and his people, because they hunt these animals for meat and oil. But the sheer number of belugas convinced him he should contact the local fishing authorities.

When the authorities arrived on the scene, they were shocked to see that almost 3,000 belugas, about one-tenth of the world's population, lay trapped by a giant wall of pack ice 18 miles long and 11 miles wide. The whales already were packed in remarkably close, and worsening weather threatened to freeze the small breathing holes that were left. The belugas continued to signal their distress with sounds of clicking, whistling, and moaning.

The variety of sounds emitted by belugas has earned them the nickname "sea canaries." These snow-white whales live in shallow waters in and near the Arctic and for eons have been an important source of meat and oil for the people of that region, including the Chukchi.

The local authorities theorized that the animals became trapped after pursuing a shoal of cod into the shallow inlet and lingered too long, unaware of the rapidly falling temperature. The situation was too much for the local people to handle, so they cabled Moscow for help: VLADIVOSTOK. FAR

Trapped belugas struggle to breathe at an air hole, or savssat, *in the Soviet Arctic.*

EASTERN SHIPPING LINES. LARGE HERD WHITE WHALES TRAPPED IN ICE BERING SEA. DUE TO ADVERSE WEATHER CONDITIONS WATER OPENINGS GETTING ALARMINGLY SMALL. POSSIBILITY OF MASS DEATH OF ANIMALS. REQUEST URGENT CONSIDERATION OF POSSIBILITY OF SENDING MOSKVA ICEBREAKER TO FREE ANIMALS.

Moscow responded immediately, dispatching the icebreaker as well as several helicopters containing a team of marine mammalogists to watch the condition of the animals, hydrologists to review ice conditions in the strait, and crews of newspaper and television reporters.

Meanwhile, the people of the nearby village of Yandrakinot tried feeding frozen fish to the distressed whales to keep them strong. Local fishermen and hunters used tractors and snow trucks to tear away hunks of ice at the edges of the breathing holes, while other villagers chopped away at the shrinking holes with picks and crowbars.

By now the weather had worsened considerably, and through the month of January the whales were penned in so close one could easily walk across the remaining open space by stepping on their bulbous white heads. Pressed together in this manner, the hapless mammals struggled to breathe; the adults lifted their calves to the surface above the crush of white bodies.

As January gave way to the bitter winds of February, the temperature dipped even further and the ice floes slowly froze together, forming a solid blanket of ice several feet thick. Open water now lay more than 10 miles distant, much too far for the belugas to chance a swim to freedom under the ice. (They can dive for only about 20 minutes even at their full strength.)

Even if the *Moskva* could create a path to open water, Soviet scientists monitoring the situation were unsure whether the belugas would follow the ship to freedom. They drew hope from a similar situation years before when some killer whales trapped by ice in Korf Bay swam through an ice-free passageway made by a ship. The powerful orcas had surfaced with gaping jaws, grasped the edges of the ice floes, and pushed them aside as they swam to freedom. Perhaps, thought the scientists, the belugas would do the same — that is, if the ship could get through the ice.

After a lengthy journey, the *Moskva* finally arrived on the scene in early February only to be confronted by ice stretching miles into the distance. In worsening weather, Captain Anatoly Kovalenko began driving his ship into the 12-foot-thick ice. Any passage opened was almost immediately frozen over, creating the dangerous possibility that even the ship itself would become icebound. Progress was extremely slow: In one four-hour period, the *Moskva* advanced less than a few hundred feet. Twice during the following hours, the captain ordered his ship to turn back in the face of the spectacular walls of ice that threatened to crush the vessel.

Professor Alfred Antonovich Berezin, director of the Laboratory of Cetaceans at the USSR's Pacific Research Institute of Fisheries and Oceanography, was monitoring the situation and urged Kovalenko on. "The operation you are conducting is very important," Berezin cabled. "We have to try to make a passage in the ice . . . you'll make things much easier for the animals."

After another two days, however, it became clear the icebreaker was not going to make it. Fuel and water reserves were running extremely low, increasing the danger of entrapment. Kovalenko ordered the *Moskva* to turn back and head for port.

The rescue of the whales — dubbed Operation Beluga by the Soviet press —had reached a critical phase. Rescue workers continued clearing ice at the breathing holes, and the whales, which had been frightened by the approach of humans in December and early January, now accepted their presence with increasing calm, whining and chirping as if, as one Soviet report noted, "signaling with their whines that people were their only hope for survival." After more than a month of entrapment, the old and weak whales started dying.

Sailors played classical music from the bridge of the Soviet icebreaker Moskva *to lure the trapped belugas to open water.*

Without a second attempt by the icebreaker, it was clear the belugas had no chance for survival. Again, authorities cabled Moscow: RESCUE MEASURES PROVE INEFFECTIVE. ANIMALS DYING. DANGER OF TOTAL LOSS. REQUEST URGENT RPT URGENT INSTRUCTIONS FOR RESCUE OF MAMMALS BY ICEBREAKER OF FAR EASTERN SHIPPING LINES.

The *Moskva* was again ordered to the scene and after taking on a full load of coal, headed for the strait. Arriving in mid-February, the ship and its crew began to attack the ice again. This time, aided by the added weight of the coal and a reconnaissance plane sent from nearby Magadan to lead the ship along the easiest route, the *Moskva* was successful, although its task was hindered by the presence of shoals in water where large ships had never operated.

Finally, on February 22, the ship reached the whales, leaving behind it a 12-mile channel to unfrozen water. At first the belugas wouldn't move. They were so exhausted by the ordeal that sailors from the *Moskva* were able to walk to the edge of the ice and pat them on the head. As the whales rested and fed in the newly opened patches of water, they slowly regained their strength and began frolicking with obvious pleasure, sometimes even hiding mischievously from the rescuers. But ghastly weather conditions persisted, slowly freezing over the open channel, and if the whales couldn't be enticed toward open water soon, the rescue effort would prove fruitless.

The whales seemed to be afraid of the icebreaker and its engine noise, so for the next four days Kovalenko and his crew tried to accustom the animals to the ship, backing out and reopening portions of the channel, then returning to the herd. After several trips the whales seemed to understand the ship's intentions, and according to Kovalenko, the belugas started to approach the vessel, rejoicing and leaping "like children." Yet they still were reluctant to follow.

Then one of the experts aboard the *Moskva* had an idea. Whales displayed a sensitivity to music in aquariums and in the wild, so why not put music on the ship's loudspeakers as a lure? The individual who suggested this may have been familiar with the ancient Greek story of Arion and the dolphins. Arion was a wealthy man who lived in the seventh century B.C. Once, when returning to Greece from southern Italy, he booked passage on a ship manned by Corinthian scoundrels who plotted to kill him and steal his money when they reached open sea. When the criminals confronted him, Arion made a last request: Could he play his lyre and then leap into the sea? They granted his wish, and upon hearing his beautiful music, dolphins gathered about the ship and carried him safely to shore after he leapt into the sea.

In recent years, many musicians have played their instruments to whales. Paul Winter has become widely known for his haunting melodies to the accompaniment of humpback whale songs, and Californian Jim Nollman played music to killer whales off British Columbia in the late 1970s with a variety of instruments, including an electric guitar. Nollman once played at the same location and time for six consecutive nights, and each night the whales showed up, apparently fascinated by the different sounds. Local residents reported that

the whales continued to visit at exactly the same time and place for three nights after he left.

Whether they were familiar with these stories or not, the Soviets needed ideas, so they began to play a variety of musical selections at full volume over the loudspeakers, including jazz, military, popular, and classical tunes. Meanwhile, the ship edged its way into the channel.

Initially, the whales showed little reaction, but when they heard the classical music, they began to follow. The delighted captain slowly backed his ship through the ice, keeping a constant eye on his charges. Occasionally, there were delays as the whales would linger in a patch of open water, hiding in the crevasses like little children. Patiently, the *Moskva* returned again and again.

In this manner, the bizarre caravan continued through the channel, the ship's loudspeakers blaring a variety of classical music over the frozen sea as 3,000 seemingly enraptured belugas followed in its wake. Finally, authorities in the nearby settlement of Provideniya received a long-awaited cable from Kovalenko: I'VE FINISHED THE JOB AND AM COMING TO YOU.

After a seven-week ordeal, the belugas trapped in Senyavina Strait had been led to freedom by the strains of classical music. One U.S. newspaper was inspired to headline its story of the rescue "Whales Come out of Haydn."

From around the world, congratulations poured into the offices of the Kremlin, including a telegram of thanks from the London offices of Greenpeace, the international environmental organization, which, ironically, has long harassed the Soviets for their whaling operations.

Although the belugas were trapped for almost two months with air holes too small to allow all of them to the surface at one time, Soviet authorities reported that only 40 whales died. For the next several weeks the herd remained in the vicinity of nearby Arakamchechen Island, where Soviet biologists kept a watchful eye on them.

At first the entire rescue operation seemed out

THE SILENT KILLER

A short stretch of the St. Lawrence River just northeast of Quebec City, Canada, is the only spot on earth where beluga whales live outside their circumpolar range. Fossils indicate that the graceful white whales have lived there, more than a thousand miles from their normal range, for more than 10,000 years. Unfortunately, fossils soon may be all that's left of the St. Lawrence belugas.

Recent studies of stranded beluga carcasses show incredible levels of toxins, such as PCBs, DDT, and the insecticide Mirex, in the blubber. These toxins are so deadly that the Canadian Department of Fisheries and Oceans forbids the export of commercial fish with 2 parts per million (ppm). Yet the breast milk of one beluga contained an unbelievable 1,725 ppm.

Scientists believe that the high level of toxins absorbed by the belugas is affecting their immunological systems, making the whales vulnerable to a wide variety of diseases, from bladder cancer to pneumonia and even heart problems. In a recent interview with the Montreal *Gazette*, Pierre Beland, chief of the Department of Fisheries and Oceans, noted that "because belugas are at the top of the food chain they are get-ting all the contaminants that the small fish they feed upon have absorbed."

The St. Lawrence belugas live year-round at the mouth of the Saguenay River, which carries toxins from aluminum smelting plants upriver. Sewage outflow from the heavily industrialized Great Lakes region also pollutes the waters of the St. Lawrence. Examinations of other whale species that appear seasonally in the St. Lawrence do not show such high toxin levels, so Beland believes there's a relationship between the amount of time spent in the St. Lawrence and the degree of contamination.

The silent killer that now threatens the St. Lawrence belugas is only the most recent assault on these docile creatures. A beluga fishery began harvesting the rivers' whales early in the 18th century for oil and hides. The fishery reached its peak a century later, when more than 400 belugas were killed each year. During the 1930s, fishermen blamed their poor salmon and cod catches on the whales, so the Quebec fisheries ministry authorized aerial-bombing extermination raids, which were followed by the establishment of a bounty of $15 for each whale killed. Within a six-year period, more than 2,233 bounties were paid. Periodic hunting continued until about 1979, when concerned marine biologists convinced the government to pass a law forbidding killing, chasing, or disturbing the belugas.

Passing laws to protect the whales from gun-toting individuals is one thing; convincing large industrial corporations to cease dumping raw sewage and industrial effluents into the river is another. This must be done soon, however, to ensure the survival of the white whales of the St. Lawrence. Cetologists believe there are only 350 to 400 belugas left of an original population estimated at about 5,000 animals.

Several years ago the St. Lawrence belugas were thought to be sterile from the effects of industrial toxins. Although these belugas now are known to produce about 30 calves per year, scientists are finding about 15 beluga carcasses annually and estimate another 15 or so are never found, indicating that the population is stable at best. Unfortunately, most cetologists tend to be less optimistic, believing that the gentle white whales of the St. Lawrence are disappearing slowly, victims of a silent killer we may be too late to stop.

of character for the Soviets, who are still active proponents of whaling. Yet it shows they are sensitive to a change in public opinion toward cetaceans, and Soviet scientists certainly were aware of the disastrous consequences the demise of one-tenth of the world's beluga population would have on the species and the fragile arctic environment.

Whatever their reasons, Soviet authorities and the Chukchi natives demonstrated a humanity that spread a special warmth that winter over the hostile, ice-encrusted shores of a lonely Siberian peninsula. □

THE BELUGA WHALE

Delphinapterus leucas
("White dolphin without fin")

Approximate maximum length & weight: 16 feet, 2,400 pounds.

Coloring: Adults are all white; calves are brown with gray spots.

Food: Schooling fish, squid, crab, and lobsters.

Distribution: Shallow waters and estuarine regions of the Arctic Ocean and some subarctic areas.

Estimated maximum age: 35 to 50 years.

Description: This snow-white whale has a robust body with a disproportionately small head. Their prominent "melon," a bulbous forehead, overhangs a small but discernible beak. Unlike most whales, their neck vertebrae are not fused, which allows them to move the head freely from side to side and up and down. This ability is believed to help them surface navigate through the ice floes. These warm-blooded mammals are well adapted to the arctic environment. They are kept warm by a thick layer of insulating blubber and have no dorsal fin, possibly to prevent heat loss. They have thick-skinned heads so they can bash through thin ice to create breathing holes.

Like all toothed whales, belugas use echolocation for hunting and navigation. They are extremely vocal cetaceans, making a variety of high-pitched chirps and squeals, which can be heard through boat hulls. This unusual characteristic has earned them the nickname "sea canaries."

Belugas adapt well to captivity and can be seen in aquariums around the world. Several thousand belugas are left, but stocks are threatened by pollution, arctic oil development, the damming of rivers near their gathering sites, native hunting, and commercial exploitation by the Soviet Union.

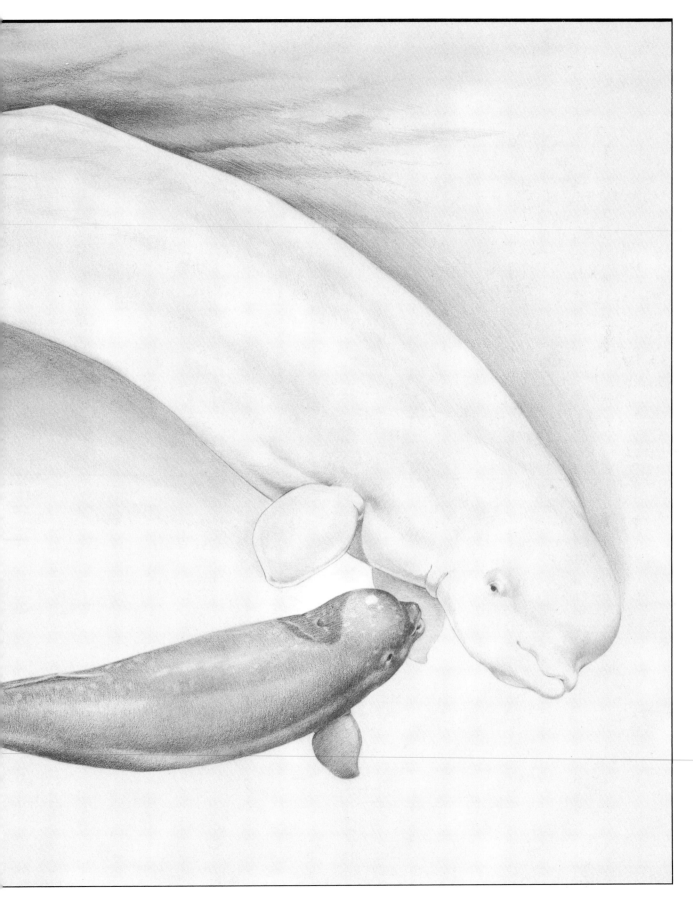

Mysteries and Monsters

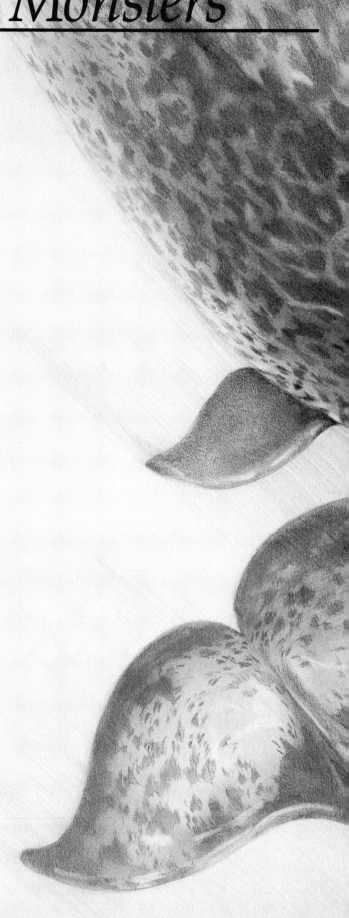

It took more than a million years for whales to evolve to their present forms, but our perception of whales has changed dramatically in just a few decades. When the first ocean explorers took to the seas, whales were considered monsters, bent on destroying human vessels. But whales also were the source of a valuable product, oil, which was used for lighting lamps, lubricating machinery, and as an ingredient in products ranging from soap to drugs. Through the middle of this century, most people's perception of whales — if they had one — was as a source of wealth.

But that has changed. To most people now, whales are a source of delight and wonder. Nevertheless, our attitudes toward them are complicated. There are whales to love and whales to fear: The humpback is considered playful and its song intriguing, but the killer whale is still viewed as a marauding hunter that kills for pleasure. Divers swimming with whales find them at one minute to be the gentle giants they are said to be and the next minute reverting to the wild creatures they are, capable of sudden violent action.

This section, then, is devoted to perceptions and misperceptions of whales and to some remaining mysteries about their lives. The last chapter will explore the greatest mystery of all: How intelligent are whales, and can we ever hope to communicate with them, to have them tell us about their lives?

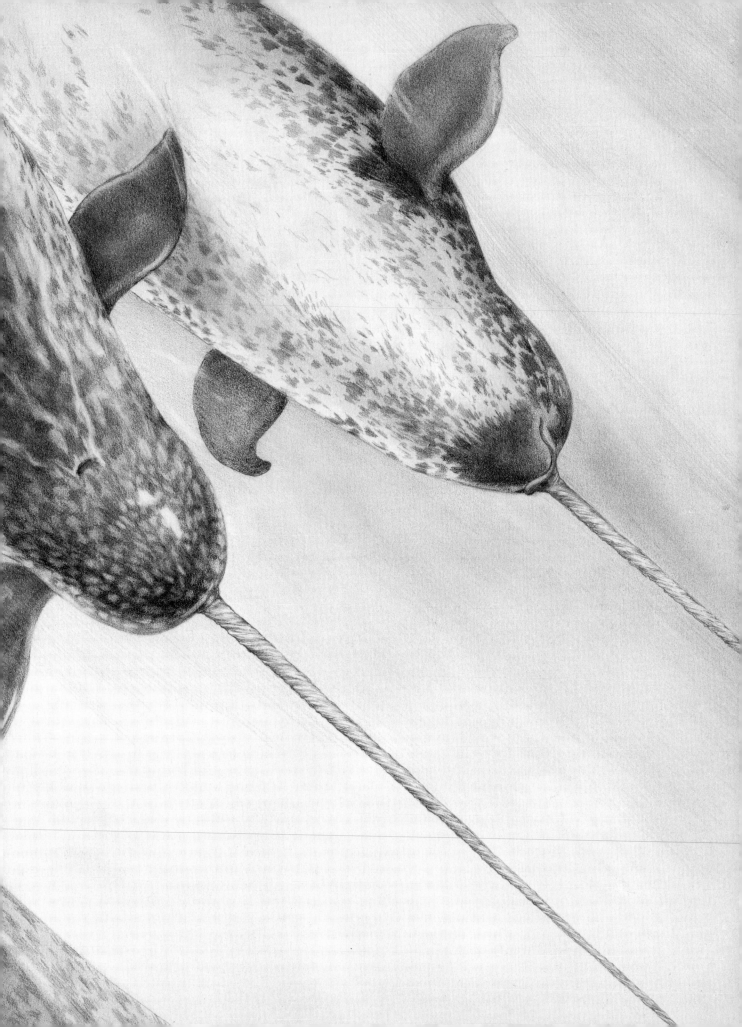

ORCA: A MISUNDERSTOOD KILLER

A killer whale cannot be properly depicted except as an enormous mass of flesh armed with savage teeth.

– Pliny the Elder
1st century A.D.

Few creatures, the white shark included, have carried as nasty a reputation through history as the killer whale. From the time of the ancient Romans, who called them "tyrants of the sea," killer whales have been said to be ferociously savage creatures, which kill not only to satisfy their enormous appetites but also, like people, for sport.

In 1963 Joseph Cook and William Wisner, in their book *Killer Whale!*, stated that although most whales and dolphins are peaceful creatures, killer whales "seem to be filled with a burning hatred." They add that "its size, power, speed, agility, and disposition have made this black monster greatly feared wherever it is known."

Reading statements like this, it's hard to believe these are the same animals that attract millions of visitors to marine parks throughout the world, where orcas kiss beautiful women and carry trainers bareback around the pool. Somewhere along the line, killer whale myth has mixed with reality, clouding our perception of this spectacular predator. Is its reputation deserved, or is it simply the victim of gross misinformation? The answer, frankly, is a little of both.

Orcas are the largest members of the dolphin family, growing to longer than 30 feet. They inhabit all the oceans of the world, although they prefer coastal waters in cool regions where seals, birds, and other prey are readily available. They are easily identified by their striking jet-black coloring with snow-white eye patches and undersides, along with their enormous dorsal fin, which can be six feet high on a fully grown male. Without doubt, these toothed whales are the most formidable predators in the sea, far more intelligent than sharks and capable of speeds exceeding 30 miles per hour.

Like the smaller dolphins, orcas utilize sound to hunt, navigate, and communicate. Each animal is capable of sending out a series of sound pulses directly at its prey. The reflecting echoes give the orca a complete sound "picture" of its victim, including size, shape, texture, traveling direction, and speed. This echolocating ability makes killer whales highly efficient predators in any sea conditions. Apart from humans, they have no natural enemies.

Orcas often are found in large congregations called pods, which are close-knit groups with highly evolved social structures. As a result, they often hunt in packs, earning their other nickname, wolves of the sea. They usually feed on fish and squid, but also eat seals, sea lions, penguins, dolphins, porpoises, and even larger whales. The many well-documented accounts of attacks on larger whales have contributed significantly to the orca's reputation as a marauder of the deep.

As early as 1725, naturalist Paul Dudley, then chief justice of Massachusetts, wrote "An Essay Upon the Natural History of Whales," in which he described the hunting methods of killer whales:

> They go in company by Dozens, and set upon a young Whale, and will bait him like so many Bull-dogs; some will lay hold of his Tail to keep him from threshing, while others lay hold of his Head, and bite and thresh him, till the poor Creature, being thus heated, lolls out his Tongue, and then some of the Killers catch hold of his Lips, and if possible of his Tongue; and after they have killed him, they feed chiefly upon his Tongue and Head, but when he begins to putrefy, they leave him.

Dudley's account may be the first to mention the preference that orcas seem to have for the lips and tongues of larger whales, but it certainly isn't the last. Whaler-naturalist Charles M. Scammon, writing in 1874, vividly described orca attacks on great whales, likening them to a "pack of hounds holding the stricken deer at bay. They cluster about the animal's head, some of their number breaching over it, while others seize it by the lips and haul the bleeding monster under water; and when captured . . . they eat out its tongue."

In the first quarter of this century, naturalist Roy Andrews, in his study of the California gray whale, interviewed several whalemen who described killer whale attacks on gray whales. One man, Captain Hans Hurum, had been pursuing 7 grays when 15 orcas suddenly appeared on the scene, causing the gray whales to turn "belly up and lay motionless, with fins outspread, apparently paralyzed by fright."

According to Hurum, the killer whale "would put its snout against the closed lips of the Devilfish (gray) and endeavor to force the mouth open and its own head inside." Andrews noted that out of 35 gray whales he examined at one shore-based whaling station, "seven had the tongues eaten to a greater or lesser extent and one had several large semicircular bites in the left lower lip," the result of killer whale attacks on the carcasses.

Recent observations of such attacks also are well documented. In 1967 Alan Baldridge from Hopkins Marine Station at California's Stanford University witnessed several orcas pursuing a gray whale mother and calf, finally dispatching the youngster. Several days later he had an opportunity to examine the carcass and found that all the blubber on the calf's underside had been stripped and its tongue eaten. Biologist David Hancock watched a pack of hungry orcas slaughter a minke whale off Vancouver Island's west coast and said after he had examined the carcass that it looked like a "freshly peeled orange."

When orcas are observed attacking live great whales, they're usually stalking a young calf or an injured or old adult, and they are not always victorious. Naturalist-author Laurens van der Post, writing about his experience on a whaling vessel in

the mid-1960s, described one such failed attack by a pod of killer whales on three blue whales. Van der Post's ship was in hot pursuit of the three giants when they noticed the orcas moving in rapidly for the kill. The mother and calf blue drew so close together "that they were difficult to separate with the naked eye." The large bull blue whale abruptly turned to meet its attackers, violently thrashing the water with its enormous flukes "like the lash of an ox-whip," with a sound that was clearly audible to van der Post above the ship's engine noise. Apparently the bull surprised the orca pack with its counterattack; it scattered the pod and chased them off.

Charles Jurasz, who has spent many years researching humpback whales off southern Alaska, once observed these whales fending off an orca attack. At first Jurasz was confused by the scene: It looked as if two humpbacks were chasing five orcas! Occasionally, they would roll over and gasp in a swirl of foam and spray. Then Jurasz noticed four other orcas pursuing the humpbacks from the rear, darting beneath the beleaguered giants to bite at their vulnerable bellies. Just before the orcas could bite, though, the humpbacks would roll, successfully fending off the bites.

Soon other humpbacks moved into the fray, swimming in tight formation to discourage the nine marauders, but the attack persisted for more than three hours. Finally, the orcas swam off, their efforts frustrated by the group defense of the humpbacks.

One of the more spectacular accounts of orcas attacking great whales comes from Billy Neelon, co-owner and captain of a commercial whale-watching vessel based in Newburyport, Massachusetts. In August 1979 Neelon and four other crewmen aboard the 65-foot fishing vessel *Ranger* saw killer whales attack three finbacks, the swift-swimming 70-foot baleen whales that frequent the Gulf of Maine.

Although only 19 years old at the time, Neelon had spent many years on the sea and was quite familiar with the variety of whales common off the

New England coast. This particular summer day was supposed to be his day off, but since the tuna were running, he and several of his co-workers had decided to spend the day fishing. They left the dock at sunrise under heavy skies; the sea was calm. By noon they were fishing the waters about eight miles off Cape Ann's Halibut Point, a traditional hot spot for tuna.

"I hadn't noticed anything unusual that day," Neelon recalls. "We saw some finbacks and minkes in the area, and several of the boats around us were having luck, although we hadn't caught anything yet. For a while we could see a lot of tuna, but suddenly they just disappeared. In fact, when I talked with some of the other boat operators a few days later, they told me that the tuna they were pulling in suddenly went wild on the lines. Even the ones that had already tired regained life and started thrashing frantically."

A short distance away, the crew spotted three finbacks grouped together, swimming somewhat erratically. Then something else appeared. "I could see about 30 of what I thought were small dolphins," Neelon remembers. "Suddenly, the 'dolphins' split into three separate groups and started chasing the finbacks. It wasn't too much later when we realized the 'dolphins' were really killer whales. It was the first time I had ever seen them in the area."

The three groups each chose a whale and surrounded it, Neelon says. Some swam in front, some in back, and several were on each side. The ones in the front and back seemed to try to block the progress of the finbacks. Then the killer whales on the sides attacked. They rolled under the finbacks and came up with hunks of meat in their mouths. For a while the finbacks thrashed around, but eventually they seemed to give up. The deadly attack continued for more than an hour before the orcas reformed their pack and swam off.

"Afterward, we pulled anchor and went over to the area to check things out," says Neelon. "The water was still all foamy and rusty red with blood,

Captain Billy Neelon witnessed a sudden attack on three finbacks by a pack of killer whales.

but we couldn't see any whale carcasses. I guess all three finbacks just sank.

"When we arrived back at the dock, we talked with several fishermen familiar with the area, and everybody agreed that when the killer whales arrived, all the fish seemed to clear right out. Even the herring seiners found the catches really erratic. They decided not to go out on their usual evening trip. It's as if all the fish in the area knew the killer whales were there."

Neelon's story offers dramatic proof of the cunning, efficiency, and power of a pod of hunting orcas, but masterful hunting skills alone are no reason to dread an animal. We don't hate lions because they prey on gazelles and zebras. It's understood that predatory behavior is the law of the jungle. So why the hatred for killer whales? The answer may lie in the belief that orcas also kill for sport.

On numerous occasions killer whales seem to have been observed playing with their prey, specifically sea lions and seals, flicking the smaller mammals about with their flukes or snouts before delivering a fatal bite. Often they then abandon

A female killer whale surfaces in Massachusetts Bay. These complex, beautiful animals range over all the world's oceans.

the dead animal.

The Jurasz family recalls watching four killer whales playing with a small seal, which tried to find refuge in a small dinghy trailed by their vessel. When the seal couldn't get in the boat, it tried flattening itself against the hull, only to be dragged under then released by a large female orca. "It was almost like watching a cat play with a mouse," Virginia Jurasz says. "Everyone on board was touched by the seal's sad brown eyes, the demands of nature, and man's lack of knowledge of how to deal with those demands."

Biologists have concluded that varying populations of killer whales display different feeding behaviors depending on the availability of food. Most of the orcas observed in the Pacific Northwest, for example, rarely are seen feeding on large whales, because salmon, a food they prefer above all else, are plentiful. Over the past 10 years scientists have identified three communities of whales ranging in specific areas. Two of these groups, called residents by the biologists, live where food is plentiful. The third group, called transients, roams a wide area of the Northwest Coast and seems to gather in poorer feeding areas. These transients seem to feed more on other marine mammals than the residents and display more erratic behavior.

What all this means is that killer whales, like many mammals, may have different behaviors in the different regions they populate. If this is the case, it's as unfair to label an entire whale species "savage killers" as it is to dislike a man because of the color of his skin.

Our historic loathing for the creatures the Germans once called *mordwal*, "the murder whale," also may be based on several well-known stories of orcas attacking people. The proliferation of such stories even led the U.S. Navy to warn in an official publication that killer whales "will attack human beings at every opportunity," despite the fact that there has never been a documented case of a human being killed by an orca.

Perhaps one of the better known orca versus man stories involves arctic explorer Robert Falcon

Scott, who witnessed a frightening spectacle while trapped in pack ice in 1911. Early one morning, more than half a dozen killer whales appeared around the edge of the ice that held his ship fast. According to Scott, the whales seemed excited, swimming rapidly back and forth and raising their snouts out of the water.

Near the water's edge two Eskimo dogs were tethered to a line that ran off the ship's stern onto the ice. Scott yelled to one of his assistants, Ponting, to grab a camera and photograph the orcas. Ponting ran to the edge of the floe, near the dogs, but the orcas had disappeared momentarily.

Suddenly, the entire floe beneath Ponting and the dogs heaved up and split into fragments. The whales had broken through the thick ice in what appeared to Scott as an attempt to attack Ponting. The orcas rocked the floe fiercely, but Ponting was able to keep his feet and leap safely onto unbroken ice; the dogs, too, were able to keep from falling in the water. The whales then lifted their heads six to eight feet out of the water searching for their prey. Scott vividly recalled "their tawny head markings, their small glistening eyes, and their terrible array of teeth — by far the largest and most terrifying in the world." Frustrated, the orcas swam off.

A dogsled driver on Admiral Richard E. Byrd's 1933 expedition to the South Pole found himself in a similar situation, out on an ice field with his team of huskies. Killer whales suddenly appeared at the edge of the ice, and aware of their reputation, the man urged his terrified, yelping huskies to gather speed. Then the chase began.

As the driver and his team sped across the ice, the orcas continually cracked through the frozen sea on both sides, poking their snouts above the water to locate their prey. At one point, one of the whales burst through the ice within reach of the horrified driver, yet both the man and dogs escaped unharmed.

These attacks may have been a case of mistaken identity. In both accounts, the dogs probably were the intended victims. Because the barking of a dog sounds much like that of a seal, it may have been the yelping that initially attracted the whales. The men involved in both situations assumed the orcas were after them, despite the possibility that they may never have been in danger. Indeed, had the killer whales recognized that they were not chasing seals — as they may have eventually — they might have ceased their pursuit earlier.

A good case in point is the only documented instance of a killer whale attacking a human, a frightening incident involving a California surfer. On September 9, 1972, 18-year-old Hans Kretschmer was surfing about 100 feet off Point Sur, near Monterey, with two friends. As he was lying on his board waiting to catch the next wave, he felt a gentle nudge from behind; turning, he saw a large, glossy black creature, which at first he thought was a shark. Before he could react, the animal bit into his left thigh but suddenly released its grip as Kretschmer hit it squarely on the head with his fist. Despite the three deep wounds caused by the bite, the boy was able to bodysurf to the beach, where he was rushed to the local medical facility.

James Hughes, a dentist and experienced diver involved in the rescue of Kretschmer, soon suspected that something other than a shark had attacked. After Kretschmer received the 100 stitches required to close the three gashes on his leg, Hughes interviewed the victim and his two friends. None of them had seen the creature until after the attack began, but all agreed that it was a "black animal that had a huge dorsal fin and white undermarkings." Hughes believed the boy had been attacked by a killer whale.

Confirmation came from Dr. Charles R. Snorf, the surgeon who did the stitching, who stated that the distance between the deep gashes corresponded to the teeth of a killer whale and that the "axe-like cuts" were "just the sort of wounds that would occur in the laceration of killer-whale-type-teeth." Also, had the surfer actually punched a shark, its sandpaperlike skin would have caused numerous abrasions on his hand.

The Kretschmer case seemed to be solid evidence of an orca attack, but a review of the facts may again prove that a person was not the intended victim. First, the boy was only 100 feet offshore, and in the confusion of the surf, the orca may have thought he had found a seal. Second, and most important, the whale let go. It's quite clear that had the orca chosen to, it easily could have dispatched Kretschmer. Perhaps the neoprene wet suit confused the animal, and after taking a bite, the orca recognized its error and retreated. Nonetheless, the young surfer survived, and there's little doubt a seal in a similar situation would not have.

Historically, we've tended to dwell on the lurid stories about killer whales, overlooking some remarkable stories of their intelligence. Take, for instance, the story of Old Tom, a large bull whale who for 40 years assisted the shore whalers of Australia. When a whale came into the area, Old Tom and several other orcas would direct the animal toward the whaler's launch. After the whale was harpooned, Old Tom would grasp the harpoon cable in his teeth to slow the tethered giant, allowing the whalemen to subdue the exhausted victim. In gratitude, the whalemen gave Old Tom the liver and lips from each whale captured.

Naturalist and author Erich Hoyt says that "when brain volume, brain convolutions, and social interaction patterns of this group of sea-going mammals are compared to those of man, the toothed whales are found to compare with or sometimes surpass man."

Biologists in the Pacific Northwest have concluded that killer whale pods in that area are close-knit, highly social groups, which feed, play, rest, and travel together all year long. They seem capable of highly complex social interaction through the use of acoustics, their highly developed sound communication in which each pod has its own distinct "dialect." By listening through underwater hydrophones to this repertoire of sounds, which includes whistles, grunts, trills, and cries, scientists

are able to identify individual pods. This communication ability allows killer whales to cooperate with each other toward a common goal.

Even before scientists in the Pacific Northwest began their studies just over a decade ago, local legends told of how killer whales took care of their own. In fact, native people of that region have a strong taboo against killing orcas. One story tells of an Indian fisherman who shot an orca and towed the carcass back to show everyone. The elders warned him that the blackfish, as they called orcas, would seek revenge, and on his next fishing trip the man disappeared.

Another story tells of two loggers skidding logs into the waters off British Columbia. One of them deliberately aimed a log so that it hit one animal in a pod of orcas. Later that night, as the lumberjacks canoed back to camp, the whales reappeared, capsized the boat, and claimed their

Although the Germans called these whales mordwal, *the "murder whale," there has never been a documented case of a killer whale attacking and killing a human being.*

victim. The innocent logger survived unharmed.

If these legends are to be believed, orcas should have killed a lot more men in revenge. One Washington State veterinarian, examining orcas captured in Puget Sound in 1970 for aquariums, found that a quarter of the animals had bullet wounds from trigger-happy fishermen concerned that whales were depleting salmon stocks.

Nevertheless, occasionally you hear a story that seems to confirm the old legends about killer whale revenge. One such story was told to me by Don Clark, a former Coast Guardsman who served for several years in killer whale country.

In June 1970, Clark's vessel, the 95-foot patrol boat *Cape Coral*, was on a routine two-week patrol in the Lynn Canal, which is part of the Stephen's Passage from Juneau to Skagway, Alaska. The 24-year-old Clark, a second class engineman, had patrolled this area many times during his three years

of service, yet he was always impressed by the rugged beauty of the coast.

Five miles north of Eldred Rock Light Station, the *Cape Coral* was steaming through calm seas when the crew spotted a pod of 12 to 15 killer whales off the port side less than half a mile away. Through binoculars they could see dorsal fins of varying heights, which meant the pod had a mixture of bulls, cows, and calves.

Sighting killer whales was not unusual for Clark and his shipmates, but this group contained more animals than Clark could recall seeing at once. As the ship maintained its heading, several calves swam over to the vessel and started playing in the wake and bow wave, much like a group of dolphins. Clark and several others stood at the rail, enjoying the sight of the frolicking animals, unaware that the chief engineman had pulled an M-1 rifle from the weapon's locker. Suddenly, the chief

A STUNNING THEORY

Scientists have known for decades that toothed whales use sound for both navigation and locating prey. But a recent theory says they also may use sound as a weapon, to stun or possibly even kill their prey.

In 1983, Kenneth Norris, a scientist from the University of California at Santa Cruz, and his colleague, Bertel Mohl of Aarhus University, Denmark, published a study speculating that some toothed whales may emit high-frequency sound waves powerful enough to debilitate prey. Their work was based on studies of captive and wild dolphins and indicates that many toothed cetaceans are able to focus their echolocation clicks into powerful pulses of sound, which temporarily immobilize fish and squid, allowing the hungry cetaceans to swim in and easily round up a meal.

This idea, dubbed the Big Bang Theory, was first suggested by two Soviet scientists in 1963, but at the time it was considered a bit far-fetched by most researchers. Norris had studied toothed whale sounds for more than three decades, however, and felt it noteworthy enough to investigate. Since then, he and Mohl have come up with some exciting evidence.

Ever since the sonar ability of dolphins was first postulated in 1946, cetologists have wondered how toothed cetaceans actually capture their prey after locating it. Because many of them feed on swift-swimming creatures, they would have to expend great amounts of energy to catch their prey. Whalemen often wondered how sperm whales with broken or deformed jaws still seemed well fed and yielded as much oil as completely healthy animals. Squid found in the stomachs of sperm whales often were whole, with no teeth marks. In fact, Spanish fishermen recently told Mohl they had observed live squid swimming out of the stomachs of freshly harpooned sperm whales.

In a series of field observations, Norris and Mohl noticed that seemingly healthy fish seemed to be unable to escape when porpoises or larger toothed whales were near. In one instance the scientists observed fish lying immobile on the surface while whales circled nearby.

To explain these phenomena, Norris theorizes that toothed whales first immobilize their prey with sound pulses, then suck them into their mouths without using their teeth. Norris and Mohl ran experiments in which they created high-intensity sounds similar to those emitted by toothed whales and succeeded in immobilizing both fish and squid. Since sperm whales are so difficult to observe at close range, the effect of their sound pulses has never been fully explored, but in 1981, an ill juvenile sperm whale being treated by specialists at a New York yacht basin dramatically demonstrated their physical power. As the clicks of the small sperm whale echoed clearly throughout the entire yacht basin, two observers waded out to the ailing creature to try to locate the sound's origin. When one of them put his hand over the animal's forehead, the force of the clicks literally pushed his hand away.

According to Norris and Mohl, the specialized sound-generating organs in toothed whales may have developed originally for communication; slowly they took on sonar capabilities as the mammals evolved.

To verify their theory, Norris and Mohl must record these high-intensity sound pulses from the animals in the wild, a difficult task because an underwater hydrophone would need to be very near the target to record the level properly. If it is ever proved conclusively, the use of sonic weaponry by toothed whales certainly would rank as one of the more dramatic discoveries in cetology.

---

opened fire, hitting one whale right in front of its three- to four-foot dorsal fin.

"It was a stupid, senseless act," Clark recalls. "We were all infuriated when we heard the shot. The CO jumped out of the bridge and yelled at the chief to put the gun away. He ordered the ship to half speed to avoid hitting the whales with the screws.

"Just after the shot, I'm certain I heard some sort of scream that seemed to come from the injured calf. It couldn't have been fifteen or twenty seconds later when we noticed about a half dozen of the large bulls peeling off from the main pod and heading full speed for our ship. It was really eerie. Even the ship's dog started whimpering and cowering like he knew something was going to happen."

The large bull orcas attacked the ship, ramming the vessel several times. Their hits resounded with teeth-chattering thuds through the ship's steel hull and cracked the ship's paint. "It was like ramming a log in the water," Clark says. "They didn't do much to our steel hull, but if we'd been in a forty-five-foot wooden crab boat, the results would have been a lot different."

The injured calf swam away trailing blood and was not sighted by the crew again. After several rammings, the bull orcas swam off and regrouped with the rest of the pod.

Few would now dispute that the orcas in Clark's account had a valid reason to attack the ship. Yet at one time the story might have been twisted to make the killer whales look like the bad guys. Fortunately, times are changing. During the past decade, as research on orcas has grown and people have seen them in captivity, public opinion toward them has changed dramatically.

Orcas have so thoroughly captured our hearts that a storm of controversy arose in 1984 when the U.S. government awarded a permit for the capture of 100 orcas off Alaska to Sea World Inc., which planned to hold 90 of the animals temporarily for study and retain 10 to stock its aquariums in California, Ohio, and Florida. The case presented a paradox. On the one hand, Sea World was an organization that had done a lot to increase our awareness of killer whales by educating and entertaining millions of people every year. On the other hand, there was a very real possibility that such a large capture could permanently disrupt the Alaskan whales' delicate social structure. In January 1985, the U.S. district court in Anchorage struck down the permit, noting that the National Marine Fisheries Service should have prepared an environmental impact statement before issuing the document to Sea World.

The issue is not whether killer whales are an endangered species. As far as scientists can determine, they are not, despite continued Soviet whaling. (The Soviet fleet recently killed 916 animals during one summer season in the Antarctic, a slaughter that in 1981 prompted the International Whaling Commission to ban the whaling of orcas worldwide.) The real issue is protection. We are only beginning to understand the complexities of killer whale populations, and a reckless use of these animals, no matter how well-meaning, could spell doom for them.

Killer whales also must contend with the threats of water pollution, overdevelopment of wilderness areas abutting their habitat, and even the invasion of their environment by whale enthusiasts. Traditionally we have been the killer whale's only enemy. The time has come to be its friend. □

THE KILLER WHALE

Orcinus orca
("Great killer")

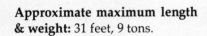

Approximate maximum length & weight: 31 feet, 9 tons.

Coloring: Striking black and white.

Food: Fish, marine birds, cephalopods, marine mammals, sea turtles.

Distribution: All oceans.

Estimated maximum age: 25 to 35 years.

Description: There is no mistaking a killer whale at sea. Its striking jet-black and snow-white coloring and high dorsal fin make it one of the easiest whales to identify. On males, the dorsal fin can grow to heights exceeding six feet; on females, three feet. These are the largest members of the dolphin family of whales and have highly evolved social structures, which scientists are only beginning to understand. Because they hunt in packs, they've earned a reputation as "wolves of the sea," and up until recently people feared them greatly, despite the fact that there is no record of orcas killing a human. In truth, they are opportunistic feeders that sometimes will attack an ailing or young great whale, but they generally prefer fish and small marine mammals such as seals and sea lions.

Orcas appear in all oceans, from the tropics to polar regions, but they generally prefer coastal areas, where fish and small marine mammals are abundant. Although growing coastal development and pollution threaten their environment, they are not an endangered species.

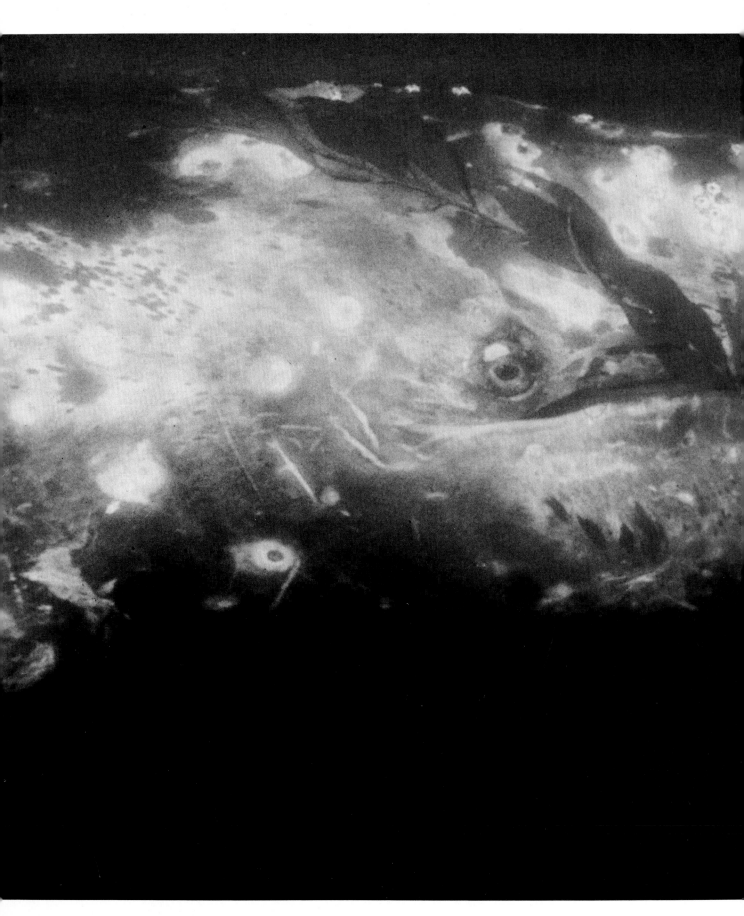

TERROR IN THE DEEP

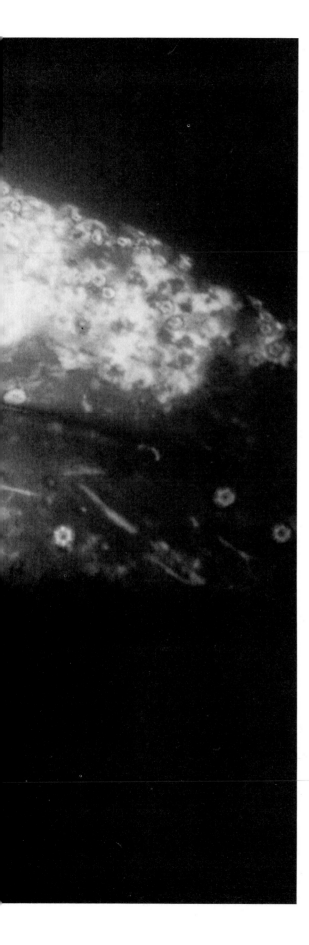

Imagine yourself in the water next to a great whale. Buoyed by the water like an astronaut floating in space, you gaze at a shadowy giant that slowly glides by, its movements timed to an ancient beat. Graceful. Elegant. In a moment or two you may feel a twinge of fear in the presence of such a gargantuan creature. The twirl of butterflies starts in the pit of your stomach and ascends to your heart as the whale swims closer. Despite their reputation as gentle giants, you wonder: Was this a mistake? Do I belong here?

Such were the misgivings of underwater cinematographer Howard Hall when he was hired in 1980 by a production company to film gray whales during their winter mating and calving season in San Ignacio Lagoon, one of several major gray whale nursing grounds located along Mexico's desolate Pacific shore. A veteran of 20 years of diving, the 35-year-old Hall has worked as an underwater cinematographer for just about every major nature show of the 1980s, including *Wild Kingdom, NOVA, American Sportsman, Survival Anglia,* and a wide variety of National Geographic specials.

Hall accepted the assignment despite some problems with the location. Since the lagoons are shallow, sandy stretches of water ripped by tidal currents, visibility rarely exceeds 12 feet, and according to Hall, an underwater cameraman would have to get within 6 feet of the cetacean to capture clear images on film. Since these might be mating animals, intent only on following their primal instinct to mate, it might be extremely dangerous for a diver to approach them.

Hall also was concerned about the gray's reputation for skittishness. Like many slow-swimming whales, grays are sometimes targets of killer whales and sharks, so they tend to be extremely wary of creatures swimming nearby. To protect themselves, they've been known to deliver power-

A gray whale feeds in the murky waters off California.

131

A gray whale bursts to the surface, its mouth bulging with kelp. The long baleen plates visible in its mouth will filter the whale's meal from the water.

ful sideways "karate" chops with their huge tail flukes, which could easily kill a diver. Biologist Ted Walker, writing about gray whales for *National Geographic* magazine, recalled one such encounter suffered by diver Rick Grigg, at the time a graduate student at the Scripps Institution of Oceanography in La Jolla, California. Grigg made the mistake of touching an unsuspecting gray underwater. According to Walker, Grigg "felt a quiver of flesh, like the muscular twitching of a horse. There was a flurry of movement, and then the whole undersea world seemed to explode." Afterward, Grigg could recall only being helped into a boat by his diving companion, nursing a substantial gash on his forehead, the result of a blow from the barnacle-encrusted tail of the gray whale.

Old-time whalers nicknamed grays "devil-fish" because of their tenacity in protecting themselves and their young, especially in the nursing lagoons. Although most harpooned whales would turn on their pursuers, grays displayed a unique persistence in the chase. More recently, grays occasionally have shown their not-so-gentle side to scientists. In 1956, when Dr. Paul Dudley White and his small crew of scientists tried to implant an electrocardiograph probe into a mother gray whale in Scammon's Lagoon, Mexico, to record the animal's heartbeat, the cow suddenly turned and charged, crashing headlong into their boat. The whale bent the propeller, sheared off the rudder, and left a gaping hole in the hull. Only through frantic bailing were the shaken scientists able to keep the boat afloat.

On another occasion, during an expedition to Baja California, Mexico, in January 1968, a Jacques-Yves Cousteau team trying to film gray whales underwater was attacked by one of them. As they pursued the whale in a Zodiac inflatable, the animal seemed to become irritated by the engine's noise, and as crewman Bernard Delemotte alternately revved and slowed the engine to keep pace with the evasive gray, it suddenly turned on its pursuers. The animal leaped clear of the water in a full breach, landing with a resounding crash on the boat. Two crewmen were pinned against the boat, while the third was able to leap clear. Fortunately, a dislocated knee was the only serious injury sustained, but the Zodiac was demolished, its wooden flooring smashed to kindling and the gas tank crushed flat.

"It's one thing to see beautiful photographs or paintings of these mammals in books and magazines, and quite another to actually swim with them," Hall says quietly. "There's a very real element of danger in obtaining underwater shots that's not really conveyed in the final footage. All the romantic prose in the world doesn't eliminate the fact that whales are wild animals with a potential for violence required for existence in a brutal environment."

Before this assignment, Hall had filmed in the lagoon waters on five other occasions; he knew the territory well. He was no stranger to gray whales underwater either: One of his shots of a gray whale feeding in a kelp bed off the California coast has run in more than 100 publications worldwide since 1975. In the clearer waters of the open Pacific, that whale had been well aware of Hall's presence, and therein lies the secret to success without danger. To get the necessary footage safely, Hall had to make sure the whales were aware of him. No surprises.

The first several days on location passed quietly as Hall and his colleague Marty Snyderman drifted in a small inflatable boat waiting for the right opportunity. Finally, three courting grays approached and started circling 50 yards away, seemingly oblivious to the presence of the inflatable. Hall grabbed his camera as he noticed one of the large animals surface, blow, and dive not 30 yards away, heading directly for the boat. As he had hundreds of times before, he flicked the safety catch off the trigger of the camera, took several quick breaths, and slid into the muddy water, directly in the path of the now hidden giant. He descended about 30 feet and stopped, waiting for

the whale. Despite the intense subtropical sun above, the water of the lagoon was oppressively dark. He recalls struggling to adjust his eyes to the darkness, able to see only a few feet, able to hear nothing.

Suddenly, great shadows swirled around him, and he knew the whales were close, perhaps too close. He squinted desperately in the darkness, trying to pick out some form, some idea of which way to turn. Instinctively, he switched on the camera and began filming, pointing the camera at what seemed to be only fleeting ghosts with little form or shape.

Seconds later a passing shadow burst through

Howard Hall at work.

133

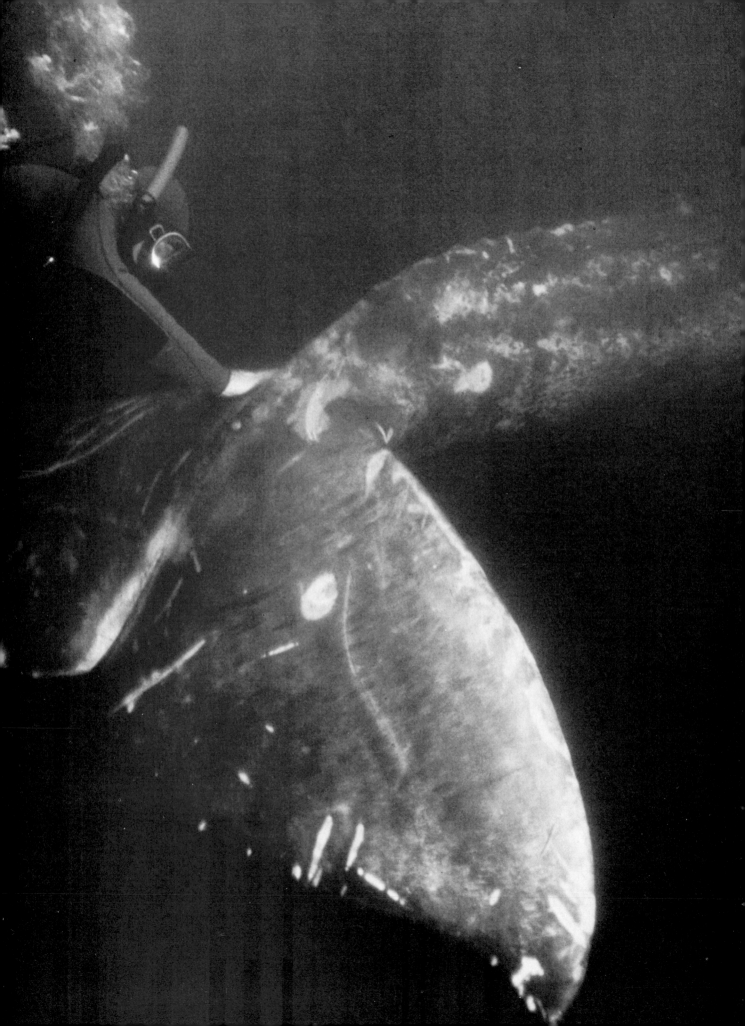

the oppressive murkiness, exposing a massive wall of flesh; the long tapered head of a gray whale passed almost within touching distance. For a fraction of a second in the limited visibility their eyes met. Hall experienced a dizzying rush of adrenalin as he gazed upon the unblinking alien stare of the giant, but his excitement rapidly gave way to a sense of dread as he realized he had startled the animal.

With a rapid twist of its pectoral fins and a jerking arch of its body, the whale turned away, clearly surprised and maybe even frightened by the unexpected meeting. "At that very instant I knew I was in the wrong place doing the wrong thing," Hall recalls. "I immediately recognized the great danger of my position. Fortunately, my gut-level reaction at that moment probably saved my life. I pulled my legs up and curled into a ball, holding the camera close to my chest. Then it hit."

When the whale hit, Hall saw a shining semi-circular white arch of light extending from in front of him to his left side; he guesses this was the vortex left behind as the flukes swung sideways. He also caught the momentary flash of the whale's flukes as they chopped with explosive force into his ribs, tumbling him head over heels in the swirl of eddies left by the whale. All went black as Hall drifted into momentary unconsciousness; then he regained his senses and instinctively swam for the surface, his lungs aching from the lack of air.

The camera, still running, hung limply by a lanyard attached to Hall's wrist as he struggled to the surface, dazed and in pain. He was helped back into the boat by his colleague, who had been unaware of the collision.

Hall suffered two broken ribs and a fractured arm, and he lost his face mask and a glove. Amazingly, in his semiconscious state after the impact, he captured the first underwater film footage of gray whales mating, which subsequently appeared on Public Television's *NOVA* program.

When the divers viewed the footage later, they realized just how much danger they'd been in at other times. At one point, while Hall bobbed at

the surface filming the forward portion of a gray whale involved in a courtship ritual, the whale's flukes lifted menacingly over his head. Concentrating on his camera, he was unaware of the danger at the time.

Hall feels no bitterness toward the animal that struck him. "Despite the fact that I know the blow was intentional, I don't blame the whale. Its reaction was instinctive, and I shouldn't have been that close."

Hall is concerned that wildlife enthusiasts may paint too pretty a picture of whales, coloring them as something other than wild creatures. "Quite honestly, I feel much safer filming sharks," he says. "At least with them you know where you stand. They have a primitive brain, so their reactions are quite predictable. On the other hand, a whale's potential for intelligence may be exactly what makes it so dangerous. You never know when a killer whale that woke up on the wrong side of the reef just might decide to tear a human apart to see what makes him tick.

"Oftentimes, environmentalists wax philosophical about our relationship to whales, saying they may be as intelligent as we are. But to say that whales have a brain as complex as ours doesn't necessarily mean they think on a similar level. When you say one animal is more intelligent than another, you're simply saying they act more human than the other. We have no way to measure intelligence on their scale. For example, sharks have survived for millions of years — they're a tremendously successful species — yet most people consider them to be stupid. We're supposed to be so intelligent, but we're slowly destroying the very environment we need to survive! Intelligence is very difficult to measure." ☐

Gray whales are notoriously skittish, but this diver was able to grasp a gray's flukes.

THE GRAY WHALE

Eschrichtius robustus
("Oaken" or "strong")

Approximate maximum length & weight: 50 feet, 30 tons.

Coloring: Mottled gray with some white and yellow patches.

Food: Bottom-dwelling amphipods, crustaceans, and small schooling fish.

Distribution: Eastern Pacific; close to extinction in the western Pacific.

Estimated maximum age: 50 years.

Description: The gray whale is considered to be the most primitive surviving baleen whale and

is the sole member of the family *Eschrichtiidae*. The whale is best known for its semiannual 6,000-mile migration along the North American west coast, the longest mammalian migration known.

The gray whale's head is narrow with a slightly bowed mouth. The whales usually are covered with numerous barnacles and whale lice, which accentuate their mottled gray appearance. Its blow is V-shaped and bushy, and it commonly raises its tail flukes when diving; it seldom submerges for more than 18 minutes. It has no dorsal fin but clear-

ly displays 6 to 12 knobs, or knucklelike bumps, along the dorsal ridge, from the midback to the flukes. Unlike most baleen whales, grays do not have numerous throat grooves. They have very thick, coarse, yellow-white baleen plates, which they use to filter crustaceans and bottom-dwelling fish from the sediments of inshore areas. Unlike most great whales, they prefer shallow coastal areas to deep ocean water.

Gray whales are very acrobatic and commonly are seen breaching, spyhopping, lobtailing, and

flipper slapping. Recently, there has been a dramatic increase in the number of gray whale "friendlies," which approach boats and allow themselves to be touched and petted.

Females calve every two years after a gestation of 13 months. Calves are about 16 feet long at birth, weighing just over 1,000 pounds. Females are fiercely protective of their newborns, a trait that earned grays the nickname "devil-fish" from whalemen.

The California gray whale has been one of the true conservation success stories of the past several decades. Brought to the brink of extinction twice within the past 150 years, it has since recovered to what many experts believe to be its original numbers before whaling — more than 16,000 animals. The western Pacific stock is severely depleted, however, and may already be extinct.

GRAY WHALE'S GHOST

Each year on the West Coast of North America, hundreds of thousands of whale watchers from Alaska to Mexico delight in the annual migration of gray whales. An estimated population of 17,000 grays swims a staggering 6,000 miles each way between their feeding grounds in the Bering and Chukchi seas in the north and their breeding and calving grounds in the warm water lagoons of Baja California, Mexico. Along the way, they swim within sight of some of our country's largest metropolitan areas, including San Francisco, Los Angeles, and San Diego. As a result, the West Coast featured this country's first commercial whale-watching excursions, which have since become a multimillion-dollar industry on both coasts.

Undoubtedly, gray whales take most of the credit, not only for the growth of whale watching as an industry, but also for the concern for whales in general. Ironically, this species not only was brought to the brink of extinction twice in the eastern Pacific but actually became extinct in the North Atlantic because of man's presence.

Clear records of the existence of the North Atlantic gray whale have never existed. The species was all but exterminated by the late 17th century, and record keeping at the time was anything but thorough. But scientists James G. Mead of the Smithsonian Institution and Edward D. Mitchell of Canada's Arctic Biological Station together published an extensive paper on the subject in 1984, proving the whale's existence.

In truth, the existence of the North Atlantic gray whale might never have been suspected had it not been for the occasional descriptions of a "mystery" whale in old natural history texts. The authors of these accounts gave discernible descriptions of many whales common to the North Atlantic, such as sperm, humpback, blue, and finback whales. But occasionally they would describe a whale whose physical characteristics sounded more like those of the gray whale than any other species.

For example, a 17th-century text by Jon Gudmundsson Laerde (the Learned) describes the whales and seals of Iceland and includes a description of a whale Icelanders called the *sandloegja*:

> Sandloegja ... Good eating. It has white baleen plates, which project from the upper jaw instead of teeth, as in all other baleen whales .... It is very tenacious of life and can come on land to lie as seal like to rest the whole day. But in sand it never breaks up.

With this description, Gudmundsson included a rough illustration depicting distinct baleen plates in the upper jaw, lack of a dorsal fin, a head small in comparison to the rest of the body, and six knoblike bumps along the top of the upper portion of the tail stock — all features common to grays. Most important, though, is the lack of any description of throat grooves, because unlike most baleen whales, grays have very few grooves. Like the sandloegja (which means sand-lier), gray whales prefer shallow coastal areas and on occasion have been known to swim in shallow surf near beaches.

The second description mentioned by Mead and Mitchell comes from Paul Dudley, a chief justice and naturalist of colonial Massachusetts, who wrote "An Essay Upon the Natural History of Whales" in 1725, which was presented to the Royal Society of London. Dudley's essay, which focused on the whales of New England, is considered one of the landmarks in early cetology. In it he describes the right, finback, humpback, and sperm whale, as well as a "scrag" whale. His description of the latter is brief:

> The Scrag whale is near a-kin to the Fin-back, but instead of a Fin on his Back, the Ridge of the After-part of his Back is scragged with a half Dozen Knobs or Knuckles; he is nearest the right Whale in

Three hundred years ago, gray whales like this one swam in the Atlantic. Now they are extinct there.

figure and for Quantity of Oil; his Bone is white, but won't split.

In Dudley's era, and for some time afterward, scrag whales were believed by whalemen to be either young or emaciated right whales. (The word "scrag" means emaciated, rough, or crooked.) There are numerous accounts of whalemen capturing scrag whales, most of which lack a thorough enough description to determine the animal's true identity. In fact, Nantucket tradition has it that the whaling industry there began in about 1672, when a scrag whale swam into the island's harbor and lingered for three days until the settlers fashioned a rough harpoon and dispatched the animal.

One of the reasons right whales could be confused with gray whales is the similarity between their dorsal regions. Neither species has a dorsal fin, and when they dive, both species arch their backs prominently before they lift their tails and disappear below the surface. At the point when their backs are most arched, just before the flukes are lifted, some emaciated or young right whales display a bony ridge formed by the vertebrae pressing on the skin, much the way our backbone protrudes when we bend forward. This ridge can look exactly like the knobby back of a gray whale.

I've observed both species at sea and can attest that they do seem remarkably similar. Both their blows are V-shaped, and gray whales may have large yellowish white patches caused by infestations of whale lice and barnacles on their dorsal region, which look like the callosities common to all right whales.

Mead recounts a similar story of whale confusion, which he ran across while involved in research at a Newfoundland whaling station in 1971. One day he was approached by Clarence George, a skipper of one of the small catch vessels, who inquired what penalties he would incur if he captured a gray whale, which was protected on the West Coast. He then described how, years before, he had sighted an animal that resembled a gray whale swimming off Newfoundland. It had white markings on its back, no dorsal fin, and several bumps on the tail stock. George had captured every sort of whale in the North Atlantic and had never seen one like this. He was certain it was a remnant of an extinct population. Days later, Mead was aboard the vessel *West Whale 8*, whose captain, Arne Borgen, had spent some time at a whaling station on the West Coast and was familiar with gray whales. Borgen was asked if he had ever seen anything resembling a gray whale in the Atlantic. Surprised, he responded that he hadn't. When Mead told him about George's story, a smile creased Borgen's face, and he recalled that he had seen the same whale. He pursued the animal and eventually harpooned it. When it was hauled out of the water, they discovered it was an emaciated finback with numerous white scars and a severed dorsal fin.

The final account Mead and Mitchell consider to be a reliable record of the North Atlantic gray whale's existence comes from the 17th century. In 1611, an expedition sponsored by The Muscovy Company of England was sent to Spitsbergen, a group of islands in the Arctic Ocean, to determine the feasibility of whaling there. The expedition's commander, Thomas Edge, was given a list of the whales he might encounter. One of the descriptions sounds very much like a gray whale:

> The fourth sort of whale is called Otta Sotta, and is of the same colour as the Trumpa (sperm whale) having finnes in his mouth all white but not above halfe a yard long, being thicker than the Trumpa but not so long. He yeeldes the best oyle but not above 30 hogs' heads.

Mead and Mitchell note that this description is "more consistent with an identification of a gray whale than with any other known species." They go on to point out that the only other cetacean with all-white baleen, the minke, would not qualify under this description because it is smaller than the animal described, is a "uniform darker color dorsally and ventrally," and yields much less oil.

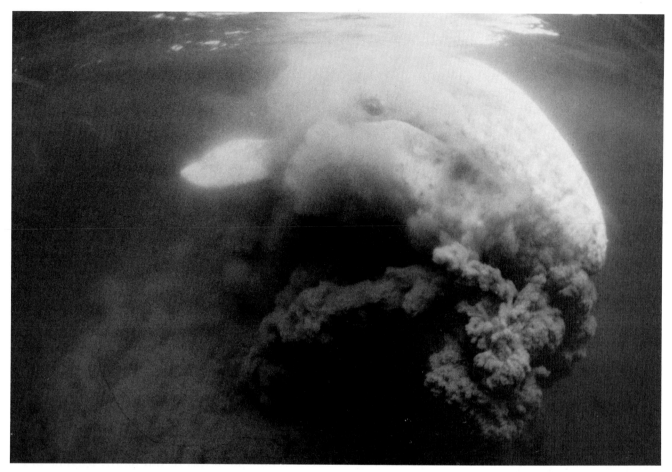

A rare photograph of a feeding gray whale, mud trailing from its mouth. Gray whales often feed by "grubbing" along the bottom for small fish and shellfish.

The most conclusive proof of the existence of the North Atlantic gray whale comes from bone specimens found on both sides of the Atlantic: seven European subfossils found from England to the Netherlands and nine American sets of bones found from Florida to New Jersey. These have been conclusively identified as those of the Atlantic gray whale.

So what happened to the North Atlantic gray? To understand, it's necessary to review the history of the same species on the other coast.

There are currently two existing populations of grays: the western Pacific, or Korean, stock, which is severely depleted from whaling, and the eastern Pacific, or California, gray whale, which has recovered from overzealous whaling twice in the past century or so.

Although Native American tribes had pursued Pacific gray whales for food and oil for centuries, the true destruction of the stock began when the Connecticut ships *Hibernia* and *United States* first entered Magdalena Bay in Baja California, Mexico, in the winter of 1845–46 to hunt gray whales. Although they took only 32 whales that year, the ships had set a precedent, and a slaughter was underway. Whalemen quickly discovered other significant breeding and calving grounds, and by killing females and calves, they reduced the gray whale population so rapidly that by the mid-1870s they had driven themselves out of business. Even for the shore-based whaling stations in northern California, grays became hard to find. Within barely two decades, almost the entire California gray whale population had disappeared.

By the turn of the century, grays were so rare in West Coast waters that when naturalist Roy Chapman Andrews learned from a whaling company in Japan about the existence of animals they called *koku kujira*, which sounded a lot like gray whales, he traveled with the company in the win-

HUNTING WITH THE MAKAH

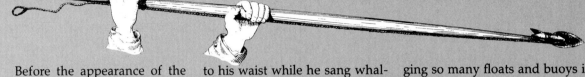

A Northwest Indian harpoon.

Before the appearance of the great Yankee whaling fleets, California gray whales were taken in small numbers by the various aboriginal tribes living along the coast. These tribes eagerly awaited the seasonal appearance of the animals, and they surrounded the hunt itself with ceremony and formality.

The Makah Indians of what is now the state of Washington, for example, put more effort into preparatory rituals than into the hunt itself. To procure help from the spirits, each morning the Indian whaleman bathed in a freshwater lake or pond until he was well "soaked." Then he stood up and rubbed himself with hemlock twigs, starting on the left side of his body; he kept rubbing until the needles were gone and the bare twigs were covered with blood. He then picked up a second bunch and repeated the process on the right side of his body. After four bunches, he was ready for the next part of the ritual.

The hunter dove below the water and held his breath, sometimes until blood burst from his ears; finally he surfaced and blew a mouthful of water toward the center of the lake or pond, making whale sounds. His movements always were slow and deliberate so the whales he hunted would act similarly. If his wife was helping him in his devotions, she would hold a rope attached to his waist while he sang whaling songs and walked around her slowly, representing a tethered whale. His wife repeated over and over again, "This is the way the whale will act!" This grueling ritual of devotion was repeated every morning during the whaling season to appease the whaling spirits and make for a safe hunt.

Although the Makah also hunted humpback and sperm whales, their primary quarry were gray whales, and the actual pursuit and capture of the giants was never easy. The Indians waited in tiny boats, their bone-tipped harpoons ready, near the kelp beds where migrating grays commonly were found. When they spotted a whale, the Indians would watch the animal's deliberate movements, figure its course, then row ahead and "lay" for the unsuspecting gray. The canoe was run up beside the surfacing giant and a harpoon driven into its side.

As soon as the whale was struck, a man behind the harpooner rapidly threw floats attached to the line overboard; sometimes there were as many as 13 floats per line. The last float to go was a marker buoy, which gave the hunters something to track when their quarry dove. This process was repeated each time the whale surfaced — harpoon after harpoon, float after float, until the whale was dragging so many floats and buoys it couldn't dive any more than a couple of feet below the surface.

Sometimes this struggle continued for hours. If the battle lasted too long, one brave individual would dive onto the back of the exhausted gray and try to subdue it by hand. Historian T.T. Waterman, in his study of the Makah tribe just after the turn of this century, wrote of one old Indian, nicknamed Santa Ana, who once dove onto the back of a badly wounded whale and, by clinging to the scores of attached lines and harpoons, dispatched the giant with a butcher knife. Every time the animal dove, Santa Ana went with him, stabbing him as best he could. Amazingly, the Indian lived to hunt many other whales.

After the whale died, a crew member dove to attach a small line to the whale's lower jaw. The line was passed through the animal's upper lip and pulled taut, jamming the jaw shut so the body could be towed easily. Additional floats were then added to the carcass to help keep it afloat. The Indians towed the body back to the village, where it was cut up and distributed with much ceremony and ritual.

In this elaborate fashion, the Indians of the West Coast hunted the gray whale. Obviously, chances are they failed more often than they succeeded, so their effect on the overall population of grays probably was minimal.

A spyhopping gray whale with its barnacled snout.

ter of 1911–12 to the south coast of Korea. He describes his first sight of a gray whale killed by the whalers: "When the winch began slowly to lift the huge black body out of the water, a very short examination told me that the 'koku kujira' really was the long-lost gray whale."

Despite the fact that Andrews had to travel all the way to Korea to catch a glimpse of a gray whale, the California stock somehow survived the initial slaughter and began to make a comeback. Then, in the late 1920s, with the onset of steam- and diesel-powered whaling vessels, they became targets again. Fortunately, the slaughter wasn't quite as devastating this time, but it was thorough enough to prompt the United States to enact a law protecting the species. Eventually, through ratification of the 1946 International Convention for the Regulation of Whaling, gray whales were protected worldwide. Amazingly, they have since recovered to what scientists believe may be the original population.

Unfortunately, the Atlantic population wasn't so durable. There's no doubt the Indians of the East Coast hunted the cetaceans, but they probably had little effect on the overall population. The most likely cause of the Atlantic gray whale's demise was European whalers.

Most historians believe the first European whalers were Basque sailors from the border region of France and Spain, who began hunting in their own waters as early as the 10th century. Eventually, they sailed west to Labrador and Newfoundland, where they established shore whaling stations whose effect on the Atlantic's cetacean population is only now beginning to be fully understood.

The recent discovery of a 16th-century Basque whaling port on the south coast of Labrador by historical geographer Selma Huxley Barkham and its subsequent exploration have unearthed evidence of an amazingly efficient whaling operation. According to Barkham, each summer at least 900 Basques sailed to the port, called Red Bay, to pursue the riches of the whale.

In 16th-century Europe, whale oil was an extremely valuable commodity, used as an all-purpose lubricant, a primary source of light, a drug additive, and the vital ingredient in scores of products ranging from soap to pitch. At the time, a 55-gallon drum of whale oil sold for the equivalent of $4,000 to $6,000. After the particularly disastrous whaling winter of 1574–75, the price per barrel was estimated at about $10,000. Even at normal prices, the average Basque ship departing Red Bay carried about 55,000 gallons of whale oil with an estimated value of between $4 million and $6 million. Thus whales became a lucrative target long before the arrival of the American colonists. Because of the inshore distribution of gray whales, it's safe to presume that the Basques, as well as Norse whalers who also operated in the area, killed most of the North Atlantic gray whales.

In a recent correspondence with Dr. Mead at the Smithsonian, I asked him whether there were any estimates of the original numbers of the North Atlantic gray whale population. He replied, "You have hit on the real question that one faces when trying to assess the history of the Atlantic gray whale population, and that is, we do not have any idea what the original population size was. It could easily have been much less than that in the Pacific. The Atlantic does not have a wide, shallow, highly productive [feeding] area in the Arctic that corresponds to the Bering and Chukchi Seas." Dr. Mead also believes the California gray was able to survive because the harsh environment of the Baja lagoons would not support native hunters, and so gray whales were able to continue breeding and calving there.

The few lone Atlantic grays that may have existed when the British colonists arrived on our coast probably were finished off ingloriously, their killers little aware that they had helped destroy a species. According to Mead and Mitchell, radiocarbon dates show that the last Atlantic gray whale probably died around 1675. □

THE SEA UNICORN

Eighteenth-century illustration of a sea unicorn.

For centuries, Europeans believed wholeheartedly that a mysterious terrestrial animal called the unicorn lived somewhere in Asia or Africa. A gleaming white horse with a single horn protruding from its forehead, the unicorn was so swift and tireless that armies of hunters could never capture it; so powerful and fierce that even the bravest soldier would dare not approach it. Yet it was vulnerable because it was hopelessly attracted to virgins. If a virgin sat near it, the unicorn would meekly approach, lay its horn in her lap, and fall into a deep sleep. Thus it *could* be captured, but, strangely, no unicorn ever was.

The unicorn was a myth that sprang from an arctic whale that exists today: the narwhal (pronounced nar-whale). The narwhal was the source of the beautiful spiraled tusks brought to Europe by the Vikings, which were said to be the horns of unicorns. (To preserve their value, the Norsemen never shared the secret origin of the tusks.)

The Middle Ages was a superstitious time, and people attributed great powers to these "magical" horns. They were said to heal the sick, prevent disease, and counteract the deadly effects of poison. Because of their value, only individuals of great power and wealth could own them. One Holy Roman emperor paid off a debt equivalent to a million dollars with two unicorn horns.

The true origin of the horns finally was discovered in 1577 by Martin Frobisher on a voyage in search of the Northwest Passage. In July of that year, Frobisher and his crew landed in a vast icy inlet on Baffin Island's southeastern corner and discovered a "great dead fish" unlike anything they had ever seen. According to Frobisher's account, it was "round like a porpoise, being about twelve feet long ... having a horn of two yards long growing out of the snout or nostrils."

Since Europeans of that time believed that all terrestrial animals had a marine counterpart, Frobisher thought he had found a marine unicorn. As a test, Frobisher reported, the crew put poisonous spiders into the horn's hollow core, since a unicorn's horn was considered the perfect antidote for any poison. The sailors must have concluded that the test worked, for Frobisher later presented the ivory treasure to Queen Elizabeth.

It was centuries before people realized that no unicorns existed, either on land or sea, only the narwhal. Nevertheless, the ivory tusks still were believed to have wondrous medical properties. Respected physicians of the Renaissance touted ground narwhal teeth as excellent for the heart and a sure-fire cure for epilepsy. Taking the powder internally was believed to cause perspiration, thus expelling "ill vapours by sweate." Even as late as 1734, Monsieur Pomet, chief druggist to French King Louis XIV, noted that many individuals chose to wear the powder of narwhal tusks "in Amulets hung about the Neck, to preserve them from infectious Air."

Today, the narwhal remains wrapped in mystery. Three major populations are known to live year-round in the Arctic Ocean. The tusks are found only in males and are one of two teeth in the upper jaw. (The second tooth rarely erupts from the gum.) Spiraling counterclockwise, the beautiful ivory tusks can exceed 10 feet in length, and according to narwhal researchers John and Deborah Ford, they are used by the animals "both as a weapon and a symbol of dominance in ritual displays."

The narwhal, whose Latin name *Monodon monoceros* means "one tooth, one horn," is one of only two cetaceans, along with the bowhead, that spends its entire life in arctic waters. These 15-foot whales (excluding the tusk) are very slow swimmers and prefer deep water. Like all toothed whales, they have an echolocating ability to navigate as well as feed.

Narwhals are not an endangered species, although natives of the Arctic, who eat the meat and skin of these mammals, are allowed a limited kill each year. Until the early 1970s, narwhal tusks represented a significant source of income for the natives. But pressure from environmentalists finally forced the European Economic Community to prohibit their import. The "magic" had worn off.

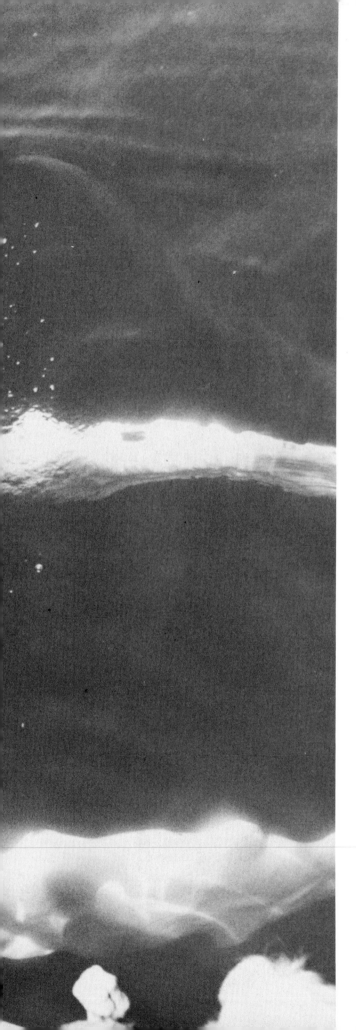

THE 'FRIENDLIES'

To the dolphin alone nature has given that which the best philosophers seek: friendship for no advantage. Though it has no need of help of any man, yet it is a genial friend to all, and has helped man.

– Plutarch, A.D. 46–120

Of all the mysteries about the lives of whales, none is older or more baffling than their apparent affinity for human beings. We like to watch and study whales because of their beauty and our curiosity about their hidden lives, but why do they seem so curious about us? We wonder about their intelligence — do they wonder about ours?

For centuries, humans have noticed that whales, especially dolphins, seem attracted to swimmers and boats. In some rare cases, whales may even have tried to rescue drowning or stranded sailors. Are we just reading something into wild animals' behavior, or are they indeed compassionate, intelligent creatures? The answer is still unknown, but the stories are intriguing.

The ancient Greeks were the first to record the friendliness and intelligence of whales. They believed all cetaceans were reincarnations of the human soul and therefore were endowed with divine intelligence. The Greeks also were convinced that dolphins cared deeply for people, which they explained by the legend of Dionysus.

Dionysus, the Greek god of wine and frenzy, once borrowed a ship to sail to Naxos, an island in the Aegean Sea, but when the journey was well underway, he noticed the ship was heading off course. He suspected the seven crewmen, unaware of their passenger's identity, planned to sell him into slavery in Asia. As punishment for their evil conspiracy, Dionysus turned the oars into serpents, caused grape vines to engulf the ship, and com-

The humpback Sirius takes a curious look at a boat full of whale watchers.

manded invisible flutes to sound, forcing the terrified sailors to leap overboard. The drowning pirates repented and were turned into dolphins by the sea god Poseidon. In gratitude for his sparing their lives, the pirate-dolphins promised to draw his sea chariot and obey his orders forever. Thus, the Greeks said, dolphins will forever be kind to humans.

Poets and authors of the classical era of Greece and Rome believed dolphins had a special affinity for children. Pliny the Elder (A.D. 23–79), in his lengthy treatise *Natural History*, wrote a famous tale of a relationship between a boy and a dolphin:

In the daies of Augustus Caesar the Emperor there was a Dolfin ... which loved wondrous well a certain boy, a poore mans sonne, who used to go every day to schoole from Baianum to Puteoli. He was woont also about noon-tide to stay at the waterside, and to call unto the Dolfin, *Simo, Simo,* and ... by this means allured the Dolfin ever to come unto him at his call . . . .

[A]t what houre soever of the day, this boy lured for him and called, *Simo,* . . . out he would come and taking bread and other victuals at his hand, would gently offer his backe to mount upon, and then down went the sharp pointed prickes of his finnes, which he would put up as it were within a sheath for fear of hurting the boy. Thus when he had him once on his back, he would carry him over the broad arme of the sea as farre as Puteoli to schoole; and thus they continued for many yeeres together, so long as the child lived. But when the boy was falne sick and dead, yet the Dolfin gave not over his haunt, but usually came to the wonted place, and missing the lad, seemed to be heavie and mourne again, untill for verie griefe and sorrow he was also found dead on shore.

An acrobatic Atlantic white-sided dolphin performs for a whale-watching boat.

Although Pliny's writings are considered mostly fictional by skeptical historians and scientists, this particular story may not have been far off the mark. As strange as it seems, it is not at all uncommon for wild dolphins frequenting the seashore to swim and frolic with bathers, especially children, often allowing the delighted youngsters to grasp their dorsal fins and take a ride.

Indeed, there have been many times during my years observing whales that I've wondered whether these ancient writers knew something we haven't confirmed yet today. I recall a particular incident several years ago that left me shaking my head in amazement. It occurred on a commercial whale watch I was cohosting off the New Hampshire coast, on one of those calm, hot days that make you wish summer could last forever. We had been observing several humpbacks for a couple of hours, and it was almost time to turn the boat around and head in.

As I stood on the bow photographing a particularly playful humpback, a girl about nine years old tugged at my sleeve. "Do you think we'll see any dolphins today?" she asked, disappointment quite evident in her tone.

I didn't have the heart to tell her that I hadn't sighted any dolphins that year, much less in the past week or so. But since I wished to encourage her curiosity about dolphins, I told her that if she wished hard enough, perhaps we might see some. I knew full well that I was just comforting her, that the chances were just about zilch, yet it wasn't 30 seconds later when naturalist Scott Mercer, standing on the bridge, spotted a tremendous herd of Atlantic white-sided dolphins racing toward our boat. It was the largest herd I had seen in years, with well over 200 animals. They surrounded the boat, leaping, flipping, riding the bow wave, and surfing in the wake.

Coincidence? Maybe. But it's a big ocean, and our boat was but a speck in its midst. The speed at which the dolphins appeared after the little girl's

request seemed to confirm the ancient belief that dolphins have a keen attachment to children.

Even stranger are the incidents of dolphins attempting to help people. Many shipwrecked sailors or downed fighter pilots during this century's World Wars told of dolphins saving their lives by pushing them toward shore. As recently as the summer of 1983, three porpoises pushed the body of a 17-year-old boy to shore at the Currituck Outer Banks near Corolla, North Carolina. The boy had been bodysurfing and was caught in the undertow of the large breakers. After his father made a futile attempt to save his life, three porpoises appeared and seemed to push the body ashore.

Dolphins appear to show compassion toward their own species as well. The Greek philosopher Aristotle (384–322 B.C.) wrote this passage:

On one occasion a school of dol-

Whale watchers stretch toward Sirius, a humpback often sighted in the Gulf of Maine. Many whales seem to like the whale-watching boats, and they often approach as if to reacquaint themselves with old friends.

phins, large and small, was seen, and two dolphins appeared swimming underneath a little dead dolphin each time it was sinking, and supported it on their backs, trying out of compassion to prevent its being devoured by some predacious fish.

This sort of behavior also has been observed of dolphins in captivity, who will support an ailing or dead companion for hours; the behavior probably is instinctive because a dolphin mother gently nudges her newborn to the surface for its first breath of air.

Apparently, the concern showed by dolphins for their own kind also can be directed toward their larger whale cousins. Mary Lou and Louis Muery witnessed proof of this on January 31, 1981, from their seaside home in Topsail Beach, North Carolina. The Muerys own a popular gift shop in the area and usually spend January traveling and buying merchandise for the next tourist season. On the last day of the month, they arrived home and fell into bed exhausted from their trip. Just before dawn, Mary Lou was awakened by what she described as "the sound of a human being in agony."

Frightened, she got up and threw open the drapes of the bedroom window, which overlooks the beach. She saw nothing in the darkness.

"I thought I must have heard it in a dream," she says. "I knew we were weary from the trip, and I thought I must have had a nightmare."

She returned to bed, but two minutes later she heard the same moan again. Its forlorn, desperate sound sent chills up her spine. This time she and Louis walked out onto the deck to get a better look. The day slowly brightened, and suddenly the Muerys saw more than 100 porpoises swimming in a tight, turbulent mass in a slough between the beach and a sandbar, about 40 feet offshore. What was going on?

The Muerys strained their eyes until they had the answer. Trapped in the slough was a 25-foot-long whale calf, surrounded by the leaping, splashing porpoises. Just beyond the sandbar in deeper water swam a 50-foot adult whale, most likely the mother, the source of the plaintive cry. The Muerys watched the mother blow and heard her spine-tingling moan, then she arched her back, lifted her massive tail flukes, and dove. They watched as the calf thrashed violently in several

A close look at the flukes of a humpback.

150

This humpback permits a whale watcher to touch its barnacled snout, a strange interaction between man and whale. Imagine a wild deer allowing itself to be petted!

hopeless attempts to cross the sandbar.

Then the huge school of porpoises moved even closer to the baby and increased their frantic circling and leaping as if to spur the calf over the sandy barrier. Within moments, the calf had edged its way over the sandbar to the freedom of open water; reunited with her calf, the mother immediately ceased her moaning.

How did the porpoises save the calf? Did they gently nudge the animal toward an unseen opening in the sandbar? Did they use their own bodies to propel the baby over the barrier? Whatever the explanation, it was clear to the Muerys that the porpoises worked together as a team to save the calf. "I was overwhelmed by it," Mary Lou says. "I still get tears in my eyes when I think of it."

The most famous friendly dolphin — Flipper aside — was a Risso's dolphin that escorted ships passing between Wellington and Nelson across Cook Strait, New Zealand, from 1888 to 1912. Nicknamed Pelorus Jack because it was always found near the entrance to Pelorus Sound, the amiable dolphin became a legend in his or her time, described by travelers such as Mark Twain and Rudyard Kipling. The animal became so famous and beloved that in September 1904 New Zealand passed a law protecting it and its species. Its eventual disappearance was at first blamed on some Norwegian whalers who were operating within Pelorus Sound, but most eventually believed the dolphin simply had died of old age.

Friendly dolphins have been known for centuries, but only in the past few years has the phenomenon of friendly great whales emerged. Granted, it isn't easy to imagine a 45-foot, 40-ton, knob-faced, barnacle-encrusted giant as cute or huggable, but some certainly seem that way. Believe me, I met one.

In June 1984, I was again cohosting a whale watch with naturalist Scott Mercer aboard the *Cetacea* out of Newburyport, Massachusetts. The weather that morning wasn't promising. Thick fog enveloped the dock and the crowd of people anxiously waiting to board the vessel. Because the

forecast called for continued fog throughout the day, Mercer offered his passengers a choice to go another day or proceed with the trip in the hope we would spot some whales in the limited visibility. They chose to go, and as it turned out, no one regretted it.

Three hours after we entered the Gulf of Maine, the 80 or so people aboard were getting quite anxious. Visibility had remained poor, and Mercer and I, along with Captain Billy Neelon, were peering into the gray mist to catch sight of a cetacean or two. We were clipping along at a brisk 17 knots when suddenly, like a gigantic cork, a large humpback burst to the surface a mere 40 yards off our bow. Neelon, no doubt with his heart in his throat, threw the engines into reverse and eased the vessel into a slow drift.

Fortune was with us, for this was no ordinary whale. It was Colt, probably one of the most playful humpbacks in the North Atlantic. Within moments he began his antics: lying on his back and slapping his mighty pectoral fins on the surface; rubbing his belly and grooved throat on the hull; spyhopping to take a good look at us; and then what I call "spraying" — his peculiar habit of blowing into the faces of unsuspecting spectators leaning over the rail for a better look.

Colt is one of more than 250 humpbacks given nicknames by Gulf of Maine scientists who photo-identify humpbacks by distinctive pigmentation patterns on the undersides of their flukes. Colt was first spotted off the Massachusetts coast as a yearling calf in 1981 and was so named because of his unusually feisty and curious behavior, even for a calf. Three years later, he hadn't mellowed a bit.

Colt continued his salty show for well over an hour, at times approaching the dazzled spectators within touching distance before disappearing beneath the boat. I stood on the bridge, camera in hand, enjoying the clarity of the water, which was

Two humpbacks feed as hungry sea gulls hover overhead, waiting for scraps.

A humpback's flukes are all that's visible as the whale stands vertically in the water.

accentuated by the grayish light conditions of the day. Then I saw it — his eye — several feet below the surface, staring hard at me. He had no doubt decided to take a moment or two just to watch the watchers, curious about the tiny visitors suspended above his watery world. Within moments he was gone.

Colt is one of many great whales encountered lately that seem to share an unusual interest in the humans that come to watch them. These "friendlies" generally seem to be younger whales that have grown up with the whale-watching industry and unlike the older adult whales, may not have been exposed to the horrors of whaling.

One of the first spots in which these friendly giants were encountered was Laguna San Ignacio in Baja California, Mexico. In 1976 gray whales began approaching the small inflatable whale-watching boats, allowing themselves to be petted and scratched by the bug-eyed passengers.

During their six winters of research in the lagoon between 1977 and 1982, Mary Lou Jones and Steven Swartz of Cetacean Research Associates, Inc., reported numerous encounters with friendly gray whales. They think the whales are attracted

Whale watchers get what seems to be a friendly visit from a gray whale. However, some scientists believe such contacts represent mild aggression. In 1983, a gray whale overturned such a boat, killing two people.

by the sound of a boat's outboard motor, which one researcher says emits noises in the same frequency range as gray whale vocalizations.

Once near, the whales seemed to enjoy being scratched on the head and upper jaw. Some of the giants remained with the boat for hours at a time, sometimes lifting the tiny craft out of the water with their heads. They even waited for the scientists to return from water too shallow for the grays to swim. One female gray placed herself beneath the boat every time it approached a sandbar and gently carried it back to the deeper water of the channel. She did this not once but five times in one hour! At other times whales would announce their presence by blowing bubbles beneath the boat. If the researchers revved the inflatable's engine, they could elicit additional bubble-bursts from the playful cetaceans.

Cautious scientists hesitate to label such behavior as friendly; they prefer to call it curious.

They believe "friendly" is a term related to human behavior, something by which we measure our world, not theirs. Other researchers feel "friendly" behavior may be a form of mild aggression. Such scientists often cite an incident that occurred in Mexico's Scammon's Lagoon in February 1983, when a small whale-watching boat suddenly was overturned by a gray whale, killing two people. Still, this isolated incident seems to have been an exception to the rule.

Indeed, there have been unsolicited encounters with great whales in areas devoid of commercial whale watching that even the most skeptical scientists have to term as friendly. For instance, in an area not too far from Pelorus Jack's old haunting grounds near Cook Strait in New Zealand, several fishermen enjoyed a spectacularly unusual diversion from their daily chores in November 1980. As the 75-foot purse seiner *Pirimai* cruised the waters near Kaikoura Beach, the vessel was repeatedly approached by a 45-foot southern right whale, which according to Captain Chris Sharp, was trying "to make contact" with the crewmen.

The inquisitive right whale repeatedly poked its head out of the water, exposing its huge eye in what looked to be a close inspection of the old wooden boat and its crew. After several close passes within touching distance, Sharp felt comfortable enough to don scuba gear and dive in the water for a closer look at his huge guest. Moments later, he found himself gazing through the crystalline water at the animal's huge eye. "We just stared at each other," he said in an interview with a local newspaper. "My heart was thumping."

As Sharp grew more relaxed in the presence of the whale, he approached so close that the whale had to lift its large tail to avoid hitting the en-thralled diver. When the rest of the *Pirimai's* crew saw this, their fear dissipated, and they all hopped into the water. One man climbed up on the animal to hitch a ride astride its slippery black back. Another crewman was lifted gently out of the water by the mammal's broad, triangular tail. "He showed absolutely no aggression and made no sudden movements, even when we jumped from the deck into the water right next to him or climbed on him," Sharp said. This bizarre encounter continued for some time, pausing occasionally when the whale seemed to get bored and swam away, only to return later to play once again.

With stories like this, it isn't difficult to understand why people are so fascinated by whales. □

A humpback lies on its side, its pectoral fin fully extended toward the sky. Scientists have no explanation for this behavior.

GIGI GOES TO SEA WORLD

No one really knows why many whales will approach whale-watching vessels so passengers can touch and stroke them, but we know exactly why *one* gray whale in the eastern Pacific is so friendly. She's Gigi, a gray who was borrowed from her home in the sea for a year-long study by scientists at Sea World in San Diego, California.

It all began in the fall of 1970, when scientists from the University of California and Sea World made public their plans to capture and study a baby gray whale. There was intense discussion within the scientific community about the wisdom of removing a calf from its mother, but most felt that the opportunity to study a baleen whale's rate of growth, blood composition, breathing patterns, feeding habits, and ability to generate sound would outweigh the dangers. After securing permission from the U.S. and Mexican governments, preparations were made.

On March 13, 1971, two Sea World vessels cruised the gray whale breeding and calving grounds in Scammon's Lagoon in Baja California, Mexico, searching for the right calf to capture. Before long, a curious mother and calf pair approached. The boat's engine roared to a start as the chase commenced. The mother and her newborn tried to outmaneuver the vessel, but the calf could submerge only briefly and was far too slow to outrun the boat. Eventually, the scientists were able to slip a noose over the calf's head and down to the base of her tail. Struggling, she towed the boat for a short time before

finally giving in to exhaustion. Shortly afterward she was loaded into a specially cushioned bait tank for the three-day journey to San Diego.

The vessel was greeted onshore by crowds of reporters and interested onlookers as the calf, now nicknamed Gigi, was measured and weighed at 18 feet long and 4,300 pounds. Then she was carefully lowered into a 50,000-gallon holding tank in a quiet section of Sea World. Officials hoped to allow the animal some peaceful time to adjust to her new home.

To feed Gigi, veterinarians concocted a special mixture designed to mimic a whale mother's milk, which consisted of whipping cream, cod liver oil, yeast, ground squid, bonito, corn oil, vitamins, and water. Unfortunately, it wasn't a hit. For two weeks Gigi refused to eat, and she lost 150 pounds. The experts decided something was wrong with the mixture, so they began eliminating the ingredients, starting with the whipping cream. That was it! Without the cream, she eagerly ingested the fishy ooze. But Gigi still reacted violently to the approach of humans, and unless the problem was solved soon, the study would have to be terminated.

Enter trainer Bud Donahoo. An experienced veteran at Sea World, Donahoo felt he could soothe Gigi by slowly winning her confidence. First he suggested draining all but three feet of water out of the pool so he could enter. While Gigi lay "grounded" in the shallow water, Donahoo sprayed the sides of her tank with a hose, a seemingly mean-

ingless task that was designed to familiarize her with his presence. When he accidentally sprinkled Gigi with water, she unexpectedly quivered with delight. Donahoo had discovered the key to her friendship. Later he learned that when the feeding hose was put in the right side of Gigi's mouth, she would thrash and fuss, but if it was inserted in the left side, she ate happily. Within a short time Gigi became fond of another human, Sue Bailey, who often would frolic with the baby giant.

By the end of May, Gigi had grown two feet and gained more than 2,000 pounds, so she was moved to a roomier 110,000-gallon tank and put on public display. Since the specialists worried that she wasn't getting enough exercise, a Pacific bottlenose dolphin named Speedy was brought into her tank to liven things up. Speedy was an immediate hit, and the two mammals seemed to become fast and inseparable friends.

While feeding Gigi a block of frozen squid one day, her trainers saw a clear demonstration of how a gray whale eats. At first Gigi just nuzzled the frozen block as it sat on the bottom of the tank. But as it began to thaw, Gigi suddenly became interested. She approached the fragments of thawed squid and sucked them up through the sides of her mouth, using her tongue like a piston pump to create an internal suction.

Gigi thrived in the confinement of her Sea World home. She consumed 250 pounds of squid and 15 gallons of formula each day and grew a pound an hour.

The gray whale calf Gigi explores her tank at Sea World. Gigi spent about a year at Sea World helping scientists understand gray whale biology.

By early fall she was 24 feet long and weighed more than 8,500 pounds. Because of her rapid growth, she was moved to a million-gallon tank, the largest available. But before long even this tank was too small. Scientists would have liked to continue their studies, but Gigi's "countdown to freedom" had begun. Before her release, scientists freeze-branded an identifying mark on Gigi's back and surgically installed a radio transmitter designed to emit signals while Gigi was at the surface.

Finally, on March 13, 1972, a full year after her capture, Gigi was lifted aboard a U.S. Navy barge. By then she was 27 feet long and weighed 7 tons. Five miles west of San Diego, a melancholy group of scientists carefully lowered her into the cold water of the Pacific. At first she swam around the barge as if she wanted to measure the confinements of her new "tank," not realizing she was free. Then she lifted her flukes and dove, heading straight for a nearby group of migrating grays.

For two months the research vessel *Cape* tracked Gigi as she readjusted to life in the wild. Apparently eager for some human contact, she would surface in the midst of daydreaming bathers along the coast, sending the terrified swimmers screaming for the beach. At one point, during the dark of night, she led the unsuspecting crew of the *Cape* into restricted waters off then President Richard Nixon's western White House. Bathed in the sudden glow of scores of floodlights, the surprised scientists had a hard time convincing the armed members of the U.S. Secret Service that they were only surveilling a whale. After two months the transmitter stopped emitting signals, just south of San Francisco.

Afterward there were numerous reports of friendly gray whales in the area, but none of them was confirmed as Gigi until December 1977. Then scientists positively identified Gigi from photographs taken by the surprised captain of a small fishing boat who had spent a long time scratching the barnacled snout of one very friendly whale.

THE BOTTLENOSED DOLPHIN

Tursiops truncatus
("Truncated dolphin-face")

Approximate maximum length & weight: 13 feet, 1,450 pounds.

Coloring: Dark to light gray dorsally, white to pink ventrally.

Food: Small fish, crustaceans, eels, mullet, and squid.

Distribution: All temperate and tropical waters.

Estimated maximum age: 35 years.

Description: Because of their adaptability to captivity, bottlenosed dolphins are the most familiar of all dolphin species. Their body shapes differ slightly from region to region, leading some researchers to believe there are at least two species of bottlenosed dolphins. Generally, they have long, somewhat stocky bodies with a clearly defined beak and a tall, curved dorsal fin on the midback.

Large herds of up to several hundred bottlenosed dolphins have been reported in offshore areas, but they are most commonly sighted in pods of about a dozen animals near shore. They often are found in shallow water, where they seem to enjoy riding the surf. They seem attracted to human activity and in some areas have adapted their feeding techniques to take advantage of human fishermen. For example, bottlenosed dolphins on the coast of West Africa aid fishermen by driving schools of mullet into their nets, receiving quantities of fish as a reward.

Females bear a single offspring every 2 to 3 years after a gestation of 12 months. Calves are born about three to four feet in length and are nursed for the first year of life. During the initial six months, calves rarely are unattended and "babysitting" behavior has been observed, in which another adult will attend the infant while the mother disappears briefly to feed.

Bottlenosed dolphins are not an endangered species, although some animals are accidentally drowned by pelagic fishing and gill net operations.

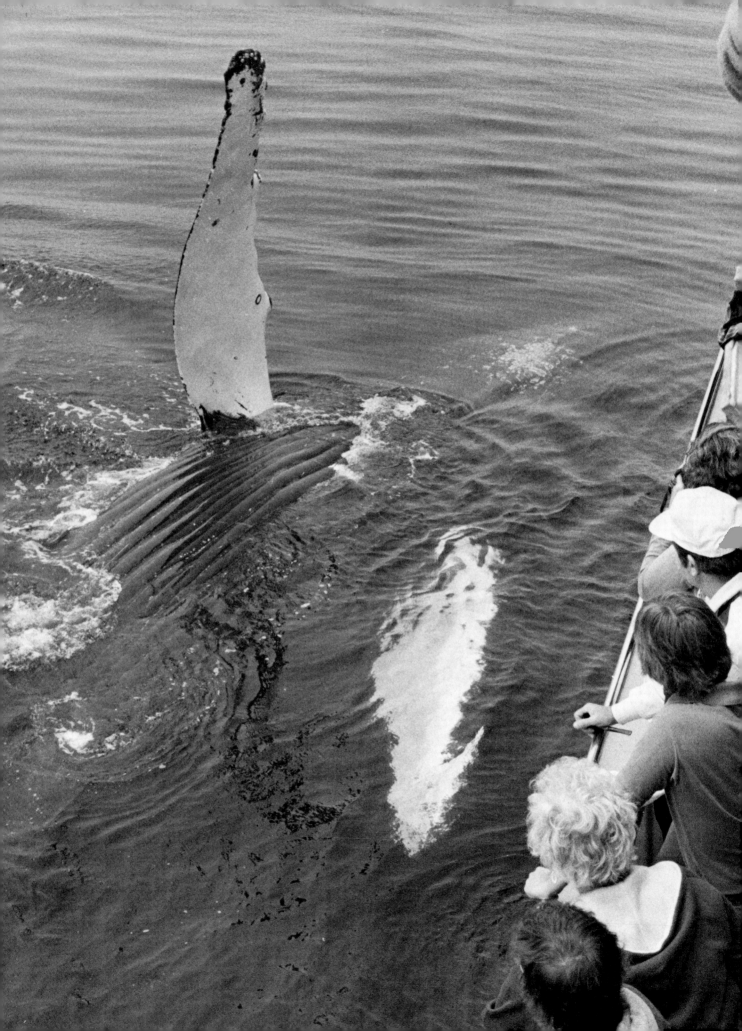

THE INTELLIGENCE QUESTION

The sun bakes the deck of a small converted fishing boat as a young cetologist shuffles along the cramped wooden deck, carefully unwinding a thin cable leading to the small underwater sound transmitter he has just set overboard. It's a typical scorching summer day off the Florida coast. The oppressively humid air seems to swell the young scientist's throat as he stretches to plug the transmitter jack into the backside of a computer console. With a beep of recognition, the keyboard monitor acknowledges the connection.

The cetologist, sweat trickling down his forehead, casts a furtive glance out the cabin door toward the clear, calm waters of the gulf. Hovering quietly near a second cable wired to a hydrophone, an Atlantic bottlenosed dolphin waits patiently, its gray torpedo-shaped body reflecting silver in the water.

Abruptly, the silence is broken by the clicking of a keyboard as the scientist types a question onto the small monitor. Moments later the underwater transmitter blares out a series of squeaks, whistles, and clicks as the scientist's question is translated by the computer into "delphinese" — the language of the dolphins.

Suddenly, the languid dolphin comes to life and bolts over to the dangling hydrophone. Pointing its snout at the underwater microphone, the cetacean returns a series of whistles and grunts. Moments later, the computer has analyzed the reply, and the scientist has an answer.

This scenario is fictional. We're still a long way from direct communication with dolphins, but if you believe the tale above, you may be one of many who consider it possible that whales possess an intelligence on a par with or greater than our own. If you are skeptical, you join scores of scientists who regard whale intelligence as fictional romanticism with no place in objective science. Either way, you get a feeling for the dramatic controversy over whale intelligence.

In any discussion of whale intelligence, it's necessary to start at the brain. The largest brain in the animal kingdom belongs to a great whale, the sperm whale. Weighing up to 17 pounds, the brain of a sperm whale is up to six times larger than a human's. It's not surprising that an animal that large has a large brain, but one of the striking features of the brains of sperm whales and all cetaceans is the development of their cerebral hemispheres (the two halves of the brain). The hemispheres are large and highly folded, which, put simply, means that the cetacean brain is well developed in its most highly evolved portion, the neocortex. This sort of brain complexity tells scientists that large portions of the organ are utilized for high mental functions.

Brain size, however, is not the final factor in determining intelligence. Other factors, such as the ability to reason and conceptualize, also define intelligence as we know it. One marine mammal specialist, John Cunningham Lilly, M.D., believes that dolphins are capable of reasoning and has long held the view that dolphins may be more intelligent than people.

In the early years of his work with dolphins in the mid-1950s, Dr. Lilly was continually impressed by the gentleness and cooperation of the dolphins, and as his work progressed, he found himself thinking of them as something other than simply animals to be trained. He discovered what he felt were indications of higher mental processes in the dolphins (primarily the capability of one of his captive dolphins to mimic human speech). About his early research, he later wrote: "We felt we were in the presence of Something, or Someone, who was on the other side of a transparent barrier which up to this point we hadn't even seen."

When Dr. Lilly published articles and books noting that whales may possess a higher intelligence, there was an outcry from more conservative

The humpback Colt raises his 15-foot pectoral fin as if to salute a crowd of whale watchers.

scientists, who felt his theories were a bit premature. Undaunted, Dr. Lilly soon became convinced that dolphins have a complicated language and that to test their intelligence fully, we must first find a means of communicating with them.

Today, he maintains his quest to cross the communication barrier by utilizing special computers in his California research facility in an attempt to decipher the complex squeaks, whistles, and chirps of his captive cetaceans. Although he firmly believes they possess their own language, called delphinese, which may carry historical and ethical information from one generation to the next, he has yet to prove his theory.

Some of the most advanced work in the study of dolphin language is being done by Dr. Louis Herman, a comparative psychologist specializing in the behavior of dolphins and whales. Over the years of his research at the University of Hawaii, he has published studies demonstrating that dolphins can remember single sounds and a series of sounds, that they can identify changes in sounds, and that they are capable of learning a symbol. As simple as these conclusions may sound, they represent years of tedious and methodical work on the way to understanding the capacity for dolphins to comprehend a language.

Dr. Herman works primarily with two bottlenosed dolphins: Akeakamai ("lover of wisdom") and Phoenix. By repeating a series of tasks designed to test their capacity to understand simple instructions, Dr. Herman has proved that the two dolphins are able to learn and understand some key features of human language, such as key words or two- to five-word sentences. Now that he has proved dolphins have the ability to comprehend some bits of human language, actual language production by the dolphins themselves will be the focus of Dr. Herman's future studies.

After all the studies of captive dolphins, which represent the primary work on whale intelligence as a whole, most scientists agree that dolphins are quick learners, have a memory, and appear to display a number of levels of feelings and interests. But the same could be said for several of the smarter apes, and the dolphin's actual capacity to think on a level with us remains open to interpretation. Dr. Forrest G. Wood, a staff biologist at the Naval Ocean Systems Center in San Diego, put it best in a recent article on the subject, stating, "With all our ability to communicate and express insights, if we cannot come up with something to measure our own intelligence adequately, I can't see how we could do it with dolphins."

As we've seen before, all toothed whales do have an ability — called echolocation — that far exceeds our sensing capabilities. This remarkable sonar ability allows them to sense the size, shape, and texture of an object, and even whether it's organic or inorganic.

This sonar ability in dolphins was first studied by Arthur McBride, curator of Florida's Marine Studios, back in the 1940s. A fisherman capturing bottlenosed dolphins for McBride noticed that when he used a fine mesh net, the dolphins would escape easily over the net's floating cork line, even at night and in turbid water that rendered vision useless. Hearing this, McBride spent several years studying this uncanny ability and finally wrote about his observations in a July 1947 paper that remained unpublished simply because the author felt he lacked solid evidence of his discovery.

Scientists later were able to prove McBride's suspicions and now believe that the echolocation clicks of toothed whales originate in the animal's nasal tract and are focused by their large melon, or forehead. Although the range of the echolocating clicks is not known, a toothed whale's capacity to interpret the returning echoes is remarkable. Some captive dolphins have been able to distinguish between fish they like and those they do not, even though the fish are exactly the same size and shape. Others have been capable of distinguishing differences between objects the size of a BB or a kernel of corn at 50 paces.

This remarkable "sixth sense" in toothed

Observing the behavior of whales, scientists can only guess at the power of their brains. What intelligence lurks behind this humpback's knobby snout?

whales has been refined dramatically by more than 50 million years of evolution, while humans have only recently mechanically duplicated sonar. As we attempt to refine the mechanics of sonar, studies of dolphin echolocation continue.

At the Dolphins Plus Inc. Marine Mammal Training Center in Key Largo, Florida, tourists are allowed to swim with captive bottlenosed dolphins as part of a research program focusing on the bond between humans and animals. The dolphins apparently enjoy giving rides to the delighted tourists, who are informed beforehand that they are "toys" brought in to amuse the dolphins.

The dolphins there use their sensitive sonar system to check out new swimmers and have proved especially adept at detecting pregnant women because of their ability to "read" the extra heartbeat. Because of the parental instinct, the dolphins often "adopt" pregnant women, gently pushing other swimmers away in order to protect the expectant mother. Once the center fooled the dolphins by bringing in a woman who was pregnant with twins. The puzzled dolphins, which never have multiple births, kept rubbing their snouts against her belly in futile attempts to figure out where the third heartbeat was coming from.

Typically, humans have found a way to misuse the trainability and echolocating abilities of dolphins. During the Vietnam War trained dolphins based at Cam Ranh Bay were freed to seek out enemy frogmen, whom they dispatched with hypodermic needles. By using their sonar in the inky depths, the dolphins would impale the unsuspecting underwater demolition experts on needles attached to carbon dioxide cartridges, killing the divers but saving the dolphins for future use. In slightly more than a year the dolphins killed 60 North Vietnamese divers and, accidentally, two Americans who got in their way. The CIA allegedly tried to sell killer dolphins to several Latin American countries a few years ago (apparently with no success), and only recently the Navy was believed to be considering their use off Nicaragua to hinder Soviet bloc ships from delivering supplies to the Sandinistas. All of which brings to mind the question of whose intelligence we should be trying to measure: theirs or ours?

There is no doubt that the debate over whale

SONGS OF THE SEA

Since humans first took to the sea, whales have captured the imagination with their awesome size and often remarkably friendly behavior. But one of their most enchanting and celebrated characteristics, the haunting singing of humpback whales, was only recently discovered.

Maritime folklore is full of tales of eerie songs emanating from the sea to lure unsuspecting mariners to their doom: The story of the Sirens in Homer's epic poem *The Odyssey* is among the better known examples. But such songs were considered myths until the spring of 1952, when Bermuda scientist Frank Watlington first recorded and identified the plaintive song of the humpback whale. Watlington, an electronics expert, was involved in a geophysical study of water-borne sounds off Bermuda, including the sounds of various marine creatures and the movements of the earth's crust. Several sets of hydrophones (underwater listening devices with ranges of several miles) were laid by cable in the depths of the waters off Bermuda. The hydrophones transmitted nonstop so the scientists could familiarize themselves with the oceanic sounds.

One April night, as Watlington sat near the loudspeaker in his lighthouse office, he was startled by an eerie, alien sound, a low-frequency moan punctuated by warbles and whistles unlike any he had heard before. After several minutes the sound faded into a distant echo, but its recording captured the imagination of the scientific world when Watlington later identified its source as a humpback whale.

In 1966, zoologist Dr. Roger Payne and an associate named Scott McVay began an extensive study of these complex patterns of sound. (They were first characterized as songs in a scientific paper published in the August 1971 issue of *Science* magazine.) Within a year, Payne's wife, Katy — like her husband a trained scientist and musician — discovered that humpback songs continually and progressively change, a characteristic that distinguishes them from bird songs.

Each humpback whale song is composed of a series of notes that the Paynes identify as the "shortest sounds in the song which seem continuous to the human ear." Repeated groups of units, usually uniform in duration, are called phrases. A variety of phrases make a theme. The Paynes define a humpback song as a "series of different themes given in a predictable order." The songs can vary in length from 6 to 30 minutes.

The songs are sung by adult male humpbacks (with only one exception noted in the many years of study) primarily during the six months of the breeding and calving season in tropical waters. In the North Atlantic they sing off the coast of Bermuda and on numerous Caribbean banks, although occasionally they'll sing in the late fall while still in northern feeding grounds. In the North Pacific they sing while near the Hawaiian islands and the Revillagigedo Islands near Baja California, Mexico. All whales in a specific region sing the same song, but during the six months of the season the songs change, so the song heard at the end of the season differs significantly from the one heard at the beginning. After a few years the song has completely changed. Each singer modifies his song to match all other singers, a fact that leads scientists to believe the whales imitate and learn from each other. The Paynes believe the whales are actively improvising, perhaps even composing.

A singing whale usually hovers motionless about 50 feet below the surface, its flippers outstretched with its head down and tail up toward the surface at a 45-degree angle. Scientists believe the melodic songs help the adult males establish dominance hierarchies and maintain floating territories, although they still don't know why the singing giants alter their songs.

One thing *is* known for sure: Humpback songs are best-sellers. Humpbacks have provided background music for numerous musicians, including Judy Collins and Paul Winter; and an album released in the 1970s, *Songs of the Humpback Whale*, lured more than 100,000 buyers into record stores across the nation.

A right whale performs a headstand as two fascinated scientists look on. We can't explain as simple a behavior as this. How can we begin to understand all the facets of these animals' complex lives?

intelligence will continue for some time to come. Whether through the use of an army of computers designed to translate delphinese, or through more mundane methods, the resolution may finally be at hand when people begin to unravel the mysteries of interspecies communication. Maybe then we'll learn whether cetaceans really do have a language, culture, or sense of history.

We do know they are highly evolved animals who are supremely well adapted to their marine environment. They do communicate with one another through the use of a stunning variety of sounds, ranging from high-pitched whistles to low-frequency sounds beyond the range of human hearing. Humpback whales have taken it a step further and developed hauntingly beautiful songs they sing during the breeding season. But whether these ranges of sound represent intelligence as we define it, we don't know.

Although it's exciting to speculate about the existence of another terrestrial intelligence, which could tell us the many untold secrets of the sea, it's important not to let the debate over whale intelligence obscure the simple beauty of the whales themselves. For many, it's not important whether whales have a language or culture, only that they continue to exist, endlessly swimming the trackless reaches of ocean, filling their niche in the complex chain of life that makes our world so vital and beautiful. ☐

A Gallery of Whale Behaviors

Since 1959, when naturalist Raymond Gilmore hosted the first whale-watching tours out of San Diego, the most common way to encounter the great whales has been aboard commercial whale-watching boats. These voyages have grown tremendously popular in states whose coastlines are frequented by whales, and nearly 500,000 people a year now view these animals at sea.

If you're not familiar with the different species and behaviors of whales, however, you may finish a whale-watching trip wondering just what you've seen. A fluke sticking up here or a flipper hanging out there often means little to the novice because it's difficult to visualize what's going on below the surface.

When lecturing on whales, I've often been confronted with this problem. Many times I'll show what I think is a dazzling slide of a spyhopping humpback only to be asked, "What part of the whale is it?" or "Is the whale upside down?" Actually, the questions are quite valid. The many species of whales display vastly different features and behaviors. Some look like sleek black torpedoes; others more like the Goodyear Blimp with calluses.

To help familiarize you with some of the ways the great whales spend their days, the following section is an illustrated gallery of their common behaviors, any one or more of which you might expect to see on a whale watch. Since behavior photographs usually show only what's above the surface, we've provided an accompanying illustration to show you what you're missing underwater.

Whales, like people, are individuals and have developed personal styles depending on a variety of environmental factors. This section of generalized behaviors applies to many and explains some of the terms (most of which originated with whalers) that are used by naturalists today.

SPYHOPPING

All species of whales have been observed spyhopping, or as whalemen used to call it, "pitchpoling." Cetaceans have fairly good eyesight above (and below) the surface, and they seem to scrutinize passing vessels, a point of land, or other surface objects that arouse their curiosity by lifting their heads high out of the water and taking a look around. For first-time whale watchers (as well as veteran observers), it is an astounding sight when the whale's massive head rises out of the sea. Since the ever-curious humpback has a penchant for spyhopping near whale-watching vessels, more than one boatload of delighted individuals has had the opportunity to scratch the barnacled chin of a whale.

SOUNDING

After a series of short surface dives, the great whales eventually descend for a longer, deeper dive, called the terminal, or "sounding," dive. This usually is preceded by a dramatic arching of the back, and some of the great whales lift their flukes clear of the sea. Depending on the species and the situation, whales may remain submerged for several minutes to an hour.

During a dive, the nonessential areas of the whale's body, such as the skin, flippers, and flukes, are deprived of the usual quantities of oxygen, which is sent instead to the vital organs: the heart, brain, and kidneys. On lengthy dives, the heart rate and blood flow are reduced by more than 50 percent, a diving reflex called bradycardia. Since whales don't breathe underwater, they don't suffer from the bends, the formation of nitrogen bubbles in the blood and other body fluids, which can be fatal to human divers. As some cetaceans dive to depths exceeding a mile, their flexible lungs and rib cages can collapse, a unique anatomical adaptation that allows them to withstand the crushing water pressure on their bodies.

LOBTAILING

Also called tail slapping, this antic is commonly observed in humpback, gray, and right whales, although several other whale species have been observed at it. The whale "stands" on its head in the water and lifts its tail high above the surface, then slaps it down forcefully, creating a loud smack that can be heard for several miles on calm days. Sometimes the whale will slap both the upper and lower sides of its tail many times before slipping beneath the surface. Because of the tremendous noise it creates, cetologists believe lobtailing may be a form of communication or possibly even a warning display, much like the way a beaver slaps its tail to warn of danger.

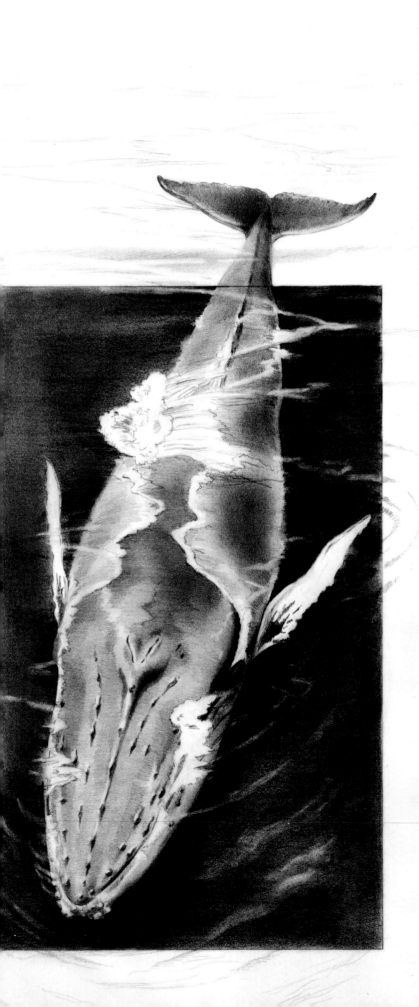

LOGGING

When a whale lies still on or near the surface for an extended period of time, it is said to be logging because it looks like a log floating on the water. Logging is believed to be a resting behavior, possibly even how whales sleep. Cetologists theorize that whales shut down one half of their brains for short catnaps while the other half remains awake to maintain bodily functions. Whales alternate their resting pattern to give both halves of their brains a break. If this method weren't employed and whales dropped off into a deep sleep, they would sink and die.

John Lilly, a marine mammal researcher, found that captive dolphins sleep for a period of three to four hours a day by first shutting one eye, then the other, for 10 to 15 minutes at a time while slowly circling the tank. Similarly, great whales rest on the surface at intervals throughout the day, barely moving and breathing slowly and rhythmically. Because they take these rests at intervals throughout a 24-hour day, whales seem as active at night as they do during the day.

BREACHING

Few natural sights are more spectacular than that of a breaching whale. All great whales breach, some more frequently than others, but humpbacks are without doubt the most acrobatic of all.

Biologist Hal Whitehead defines two distinct types of breaching: the belly flop and the true breach. A belly-flopping whale leaps out of the water almost to the full length of its body, landing on its belly, often exhaling at the peak of its jump. A true breach is more common: The whale leaps out of the water, then twists in midair before landing with a thunderous splash on its back. A whale rarely leaps clear of the water completely — usually its tail flukes remain submerged. The animal may breach only once or leap continually.

According to Whitehead, a breach represents the extreme use of a whale's propulsive power. He estimates that a 36-foot adult humpback would have to break the surface traveling at about 17 miles per hour to execute a full breach. A humpback usually builds up speed by swimming parallel to the surface, then abruptly raises its flukes and tilts its head upward to explode from the water.

To date, scientists are unsure why whales breach, but they believe it may have to do with social interaction, communication (since the resulting sound travels great distances underwater), and, in young whales, play. The more rotund species of whales — humpbacks, right, and gray whales — tend to breach more frequently. Breaching seems to increase as the wind rises, and when one whale breaches, others in the immediate vicinity tend to start breaching as well.

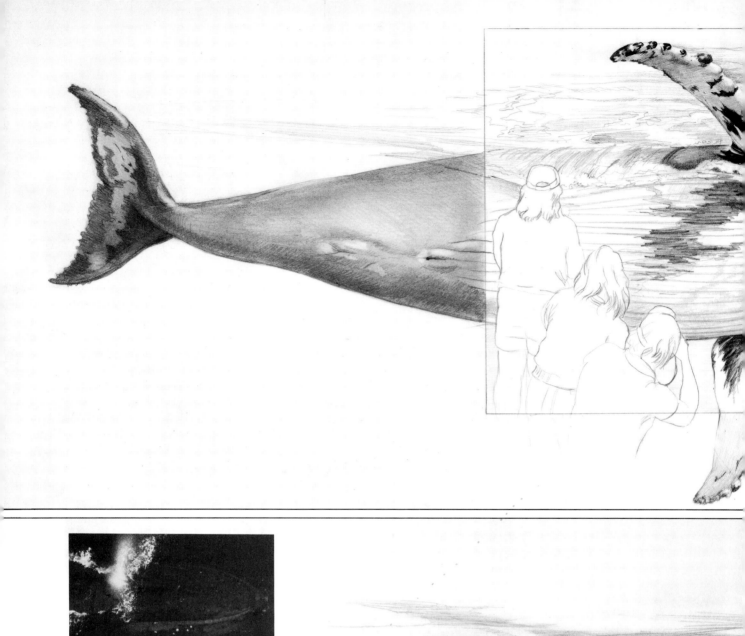

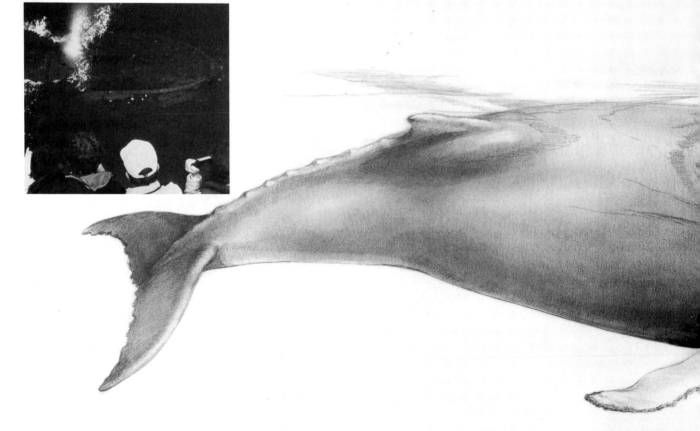

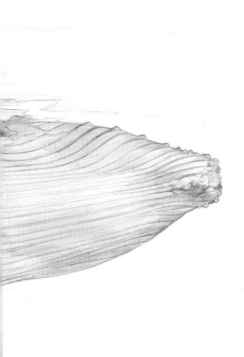

FLIPPER SLAPPING

What whalemen used to call finning or flippering is a behavior most commonly seen with humpback, gray, and right whales, although, again, several other cetaceans also do it. The whale lies on its side and lifts its pectoral fin out of the water, then slaps it down on the surface, creating a cracking noise heard from more than a mile away. Humpbacks often lie on their backs and slap the surface with both pectoral fins at once, continuing for hours at a time. The playful-looking antic still puzzles scientists, who theorize it could be anything from play behavior to a means of communication.

SPRAYING

Here's one behavior you won't find defined in any cetology textbook or whaling history, but I've seen it enough off the New England coast to feel it warrants some explanation. On numerous occasions when I've encountered a humpback nicknamed Colt, I've witnessed a humorous behavior I've chosen to call spraying.

Invariably, Colt approaches the side of the vessel and, just as a large group of people is hanging over the rail to catch a glimpse of the whale, he blows mightily, sending the atomized particles of water directly into the faces of the spectators. It's fun to watch but a little offensive if you're on the receiving end.

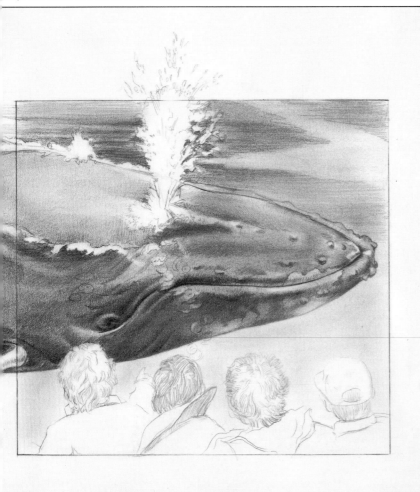

177

BLOWING

Although whales look a lot like fish, they are warm-blooded, air-breathing mammals uniquely designed for life in a liquid environment. During the course of evolution, the whale's nostrils, or blowholes, have migrated to the top of its head, which breaks the surface before the rest of the body when the whale comes up for air. Baleen whales have two openings, much like a human's nostrils; toothed whales have a single opening. When inhaling, a whale's lungs fill to about 90 percent of their total capacity; by comparison, we normally use only about 20 percent of our lung capacity. When exhaling, great whales produce a visible spout, or blow, which is not all water, as ancient mariners used to believe, but rather a mixture of gases and water droplets. Because of the great whales' varying sizes, as well as the position and spacing of their blowholes, whales each have distinctly shaped blows, which experienced whale watchers learn to identify.

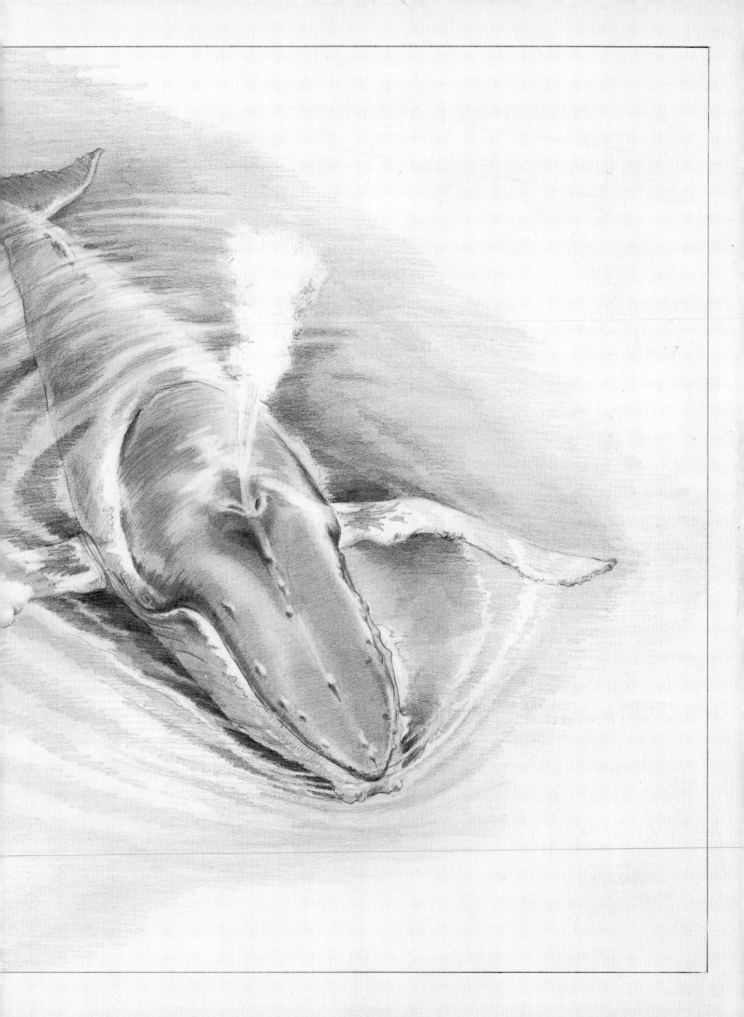

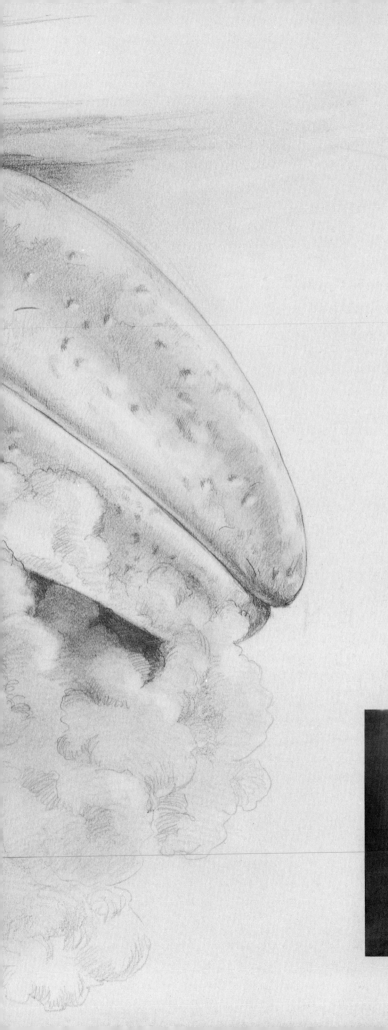

GRUBBING

(gray whales)

Although this feeding style is unique to gray whales, it is believed to have been used by the ancestors of all baleen whales. Gray whales feed on shrimp, clams, and small fish within or near the bottom sediments of inshore waters. When grubbing, a gray whale swims sideways along the ocean floor, pushing water out through its baleen plates to stir up bottom sediments. By drawing its tongue back, it creates suction to pull the sediment and organisms into its mouth. As it heads for the surface to breathe, the whale may sluice its mouth with clean water before swallowing its catch, leaving a trail of muddy water. As a result of grubbing, gray whales caught by whalers often had rocks, seaweed, and sticks in their stomachs, along with bottom-dwelling fish and crustaceans. Since gray whales are the only whales known to feed this way, scientists theorize that lack of competition for food has helped them recover twice from the brink of extinction on the North American West Coast.

LUNGE FEEDING

(humpback, finback, minke, Bryde's, sei, and blue whales)

When food is abundant, most baleen whales lunge feed. The whale either approaches the food from below or on its side at the surface. In a dramatic lunge, it bolts at the patch of water filled with food and its throat pleats expand to accommodate thousands of gallons of water. The whale then contracts its throat and jaw muscles and squirts the water out through the baleen, leaving only the food behind.

SKIM
FEEDING

(right and bowhead whales; less frequently sei and blue whales)

Because right and bowhead whales have enormous mouths with finely fringed baleen, they feed by skimming through patches of plankton on or near the surface. Their mouths remain open continuously as they filter about 20 cubic yards of water per minute for microscopic plankton. Scientists have likened the sound of a feeding right whale to a loud smacking of lips (dubbed "baleen rattle"), as the animal shakes its baleen to dislodge the plankton from the hairlike fringe of the plates. An adult right whale will filter more than two tons of plankton from the water's surface each day.

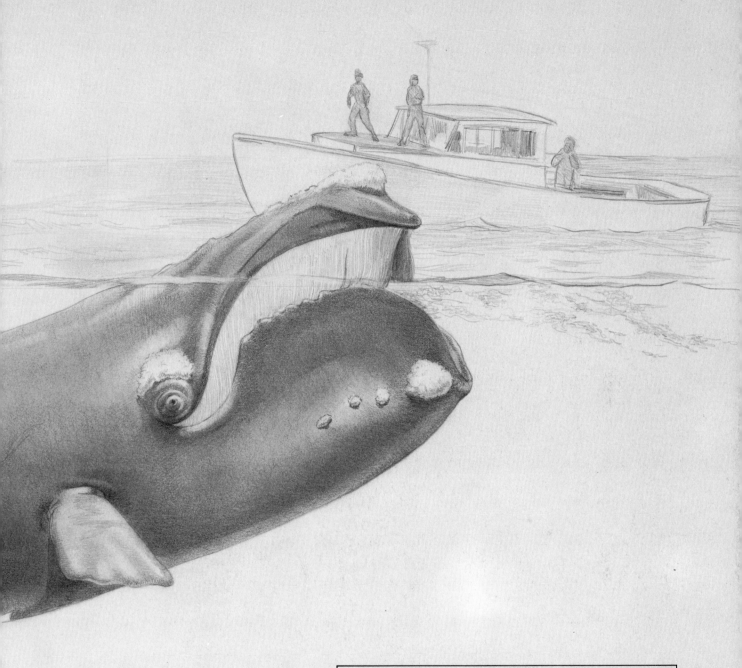

BUBBLE-NET FEEDING

(humpbacks only)

On their northern feeding grounds, humpbacks feed on small schooling fish such as herring and sand lance, as well as krill, which are small, shrimplike crustaceans found in high concentrations. To gather food in a condensed mass, humpbacks often will dive 50 to 100 feet, then release air through their blowholes while rising in a slow spiral. The resulting circle of rising bubbles creates a "net" from 50 to 100 feet in diameter, which "traps" krill and schooling fish within its center. The humpback surfaces with its mouth agape, its throat pleats expanded like a pelican's pouch, taking in hundreds of gallons of water and food at once. Sometimes several whales share a single net. After straining the water through its plates of baleen, the whale swallows the food trapped within its mouth. Using this and other feeding methods, an average adult humpback will consume 2,000 pounds of food per day.

BUBBLE-CLOUD FEEDING

(humpbacks only)

This is similar to bubble-net feeding, but the whale blows a single cloud of bubbles from 50 to 100 feet down, which expands to about 25 feet in diameter as it rises to the surface. Presumably, the bubble cloud camouflages the whale as it surfaces with its mouth open wide, gulping food and water.

186

Useful References on Whales

Abstracts from the Conference of the Western North Atlantic Marine Mammal Research Association, Boston, December 1–2, 1984.

Abstracts from the Sixth Biennial Conference on the Biology of Marine Mammals. The Society for Marine Mammalogy, Vancouver, British Columbia, November 22–26, 1985.

Allen, Glover M. *The Whalebone Whales of New England*. Memoirs of the Boston Society of Natural History, vol. 8, no. 2. Boston: Boston Society of Natural History, 1916.

Andrews, Roy Chapman. *Whale Hunting with Gun and Camera*. New York: D. Appleton and Company, 1916.

Bonner, W. Nigel. *Whales*. Poole, Dorset, England: Blandford Press, 1980.

Bright, Michael. *Whales*. New York: Gallery Books, 1985.

Coerr, Eleanor, and William G. Evans. *Gigi: A Baby Whale Borrowed for Science and Returned to the Sea*. New York: G.P. Putnam's Sons, 1980.

Cook, Joseph J., and William L. Wisner. *Killer Whale!* New York: Dodd, Mead & Company, 1963.

Cousteau, Jacques-Yves, and Philippe Diolé. *Dolphins*. Translated by J.F. Bernard. New York: A & W Visual Library, 1975.

Cousteau, Jacques-Yves, and Philippe Diolé. *The Whale: Mighty Monarch of the Sea*. New York: A & W Visual Library, 1972.

Dietz, Tim. *Tales of Whales*. Portland, Maine: Guy Gannett Publishing Company, 1982.

Fairley, James. *Irish Whales and Whaling*. Belfast, Ireland: Blackstaff Press Limited, 1981.

Friends of the Earth. *The Whale Manual*. San Francisco: Friends of the Earth Books, 1978.

Hoyt, Erich. *The Whale Called Killer*. New York: E.P. Dutton, 1981.

Hoyt, Erich. *The Whale Watcher's Handbook*. Garden City, New York: Doubleday & Company, Inc., 1984.

Jones, Mary Lou, Steven L. Swartz, and Stephen Leatherwood, eds. *The Gray Whale: Eschrichtius robustus*. Orlando, Florida: Academic Press, Inc., 1984.

Katona, Steven K., Valerie Rough, and David T. Richardson. *A Field Guide to the Whales, Porpoises and Seals of the Gulf of Maine and Eastern Canada*. New York: Charles Scribner's Sons, 1983.

Kelly, John E., Scott Mercer, and Steve Wolf. *The Great Whale Book*. Washington, D.C.: The Center for Environmental Education, 1981.

Krone, Chester. *The World of the Dolphin*. New York: Belmont/Tower Books, 1972.

Lane, Frank W. *Kingdom of the Octopus*. New York: Pyramid Publications, 1960.

Leatherwood, Stephen, and Randall R. Reeves. *The Sierra Club Handbook of Whales and Dolphins*. San Francisco: Sierra Club Books, 1983.

Lockley, Ronald M. *Whales, Dolphins and Porpoises*. Sydney, Australia: Methuen of Australia Pty. Ltd., 1972.

Matthews, L. Harrison. *The Natural History of the Whale*. New York: Columbia University Press, 1978.

McIntyre, Joan. *Mind in the Waters*. New York: Charles Scribner's Sons, 1974.

Melville, Herman. *Moby Dick or The White Whale*. New York: New American Library, 1980.

Minasian, Stanley M., Kenneth C. Balcomb, and Larry Foster. *The World's Whales: The Complete Illustrated Guide*. Washington, D.C.: Smithsonian Books, 1984.

The Oceanic Society Field Guide to the Gray Whale. San Francisco: Legacy Publishing Company, 1983.

Payne, Roger, ed. *Communication and Behavior of Whales*. American Association for the Advancement of Science Selected Symposium 76. Boulder, Colorado: Westview Press, Inc., 1983.

Rice, Dale W., and Allen A. Wolman. *The Life History and Ecology of the Gray Whale (Eschrichtius robustus)*. Lake Placid, Florida: The American Society of Mammalogists, 1971.

Scammon, Charles M. *The Marine Mammals of the North-western Coast of North America*. New York: Dover Publications, Inc., 1968.

Thorndike, Joseph J., Jr., ed. *Mysteries of the Deep*. New York: American Heritage Publishing Company, Inc., 1980.

True, Frederick W. *The Whalebone Whales of the Western North Atlantic*. Washington, D.C.: Smithsonian Institution Press, 1983.

Walker, Theodore J. *Whale Primer: With Special Attention to the California Gray Whale*. Cabrillo Historical Association, 1979.

Waterman, T.T. *The Whaling Equipment of the Makah Indians*. Seattle: University of Washington Publications, 1920.

Whipple, A.B.C. *The Whalers*. Alexandria, Virginia: Time-Life Books, 1979.

Winn, Lois King, and Howard E. Winn. *Wings in the Sea: The Humpback Whale*. Hanover, New Hampshire: University Press of New England, 1985.

Index

Photo Credits

Part I: 18, Dietz; 20-21, courtesy of Mingan Island Cetacean Study; 22, Dietz; 23, top left, courtesy of Mingan Island Cetacean Study; 23, top right, Rich Sears/MICS; 23, bottom, Mike Williamson/MICS; 24, Rich Sears/MICS; 30-31, Mark J. Ferrari/Humpback Whale Fund; 32, Mark J. Ferrari/Humpback Whale Fund; 33, left, Dietz; 33, right, top and bottom, Dietz; 34-35, Deborah A. Glockner-Ferrari/Humpback Whale Fund; 37, Mark J. Ferrari/Humpback Whale Fund; 38-39, E. Kevin Thorsell; 42-43, Flip Nicklin; 45, Flip Nicklin; 46, National Marine Fisheries Service photo; 52-53, Flip Nicklin; 54, Joe Thompson; 55, Dietz; 56, Dietz; 57, Dietz; 58-59, Flip Nicklin; 60, Dietz.

Part II: 64, Thomas Hahn; 65, Thomas Hahn; 66, New England Aquarium photo; 68, Dietz; 69, National Marine Fisheries Service photo; 71, National Marine Fisheries Service photo; 74, reprinted by permission of the San Francisco *Examiner;* 77, National Marine Fisheries Service photo; 78, map by Eugenie Seidenberg; 81, National Marine Fisheries Service photo; 82, National Marine Fisheries Service photo; 85, Russ Reed/Oakland *Tribune;* 87, reprinted courtesy of the Minneapolis *Star and Tribune;* 88, Russ Reed/Oakland *Tribune;* 89, Dietz; 91, Dietz; 92, Susan Jane Lapides; 93, Center for Coastal Studies photo; 95, reprinted courtesy of the Minneapolis *Star and Tribune;* 96, Dietz; 97, Dietz; 98, Dietz; 99, both photos, Dietz; 100, Dietz; 101, Dietz; 102, E. Kevin Thorsell; 103, John Rasmussen/Narssaq Foto; 106, Tass/Sovfoto; 109, Tass/Sovfoto.

Part III: 119, Dietz; 122, Allen Abend/New England Aquarium; 124-125, Flip Nicklin; 130-131, Howard Hall; 132, Howard Hall; 133, Howard Hall; 134, Howard Hall; 138, Francois Gohier; 141, Flip Nicklin; 143, Francois Gohier; 146-147, Daniel Viehman; 148, Dietz; 149, Dietz; 150, Dietz; 151, Dietz; 152, Dietz; 153, Dietz; 154, Francois Gohier; 155, Dietz; 157, courtesy of Sea World; 160, Dietz; 163, Dietz; 165, Center for Coastal Studies photo.

Part IV: 168, Dietz; 171, Dietz; 172, Dietz; 173, Dietz; 174, Dietz; 176, Dietz; 177, Dietz; 178, Dietz; 181, Flip Nicklin; 182, Dietz; 185, Center for Coastal Studies photo; 187, Dietz.

DATE DUE
